Linda Tellington-Jones

Getting In TTouch® with Your Puppy

Linda Tellington-Jones
with Gudrun Braun
Translated by Sybil Taylor

Trafalgar Square Books
North Pomfret, Vermont

First published in the United States of America in 2007 by
Trafalgar Square Books
North Pomfret, Vermont 05053

Printed in China

Originally published in the German language as *Welpenschule mit Linda Tellington-Jones* by
Franckh-Kosmos Verlags-GmbH & Co., Stuttgart, 2006

Library of Congress Control Number: 2007921904

ISBN: 978-1-57076-372-4

Cover design by Heather Mansfield
Book design by Friedhelm Steinen-Broo, eStudio Calamar

Illustration credits:
Photos by Gabriele Metz. Additional images courtesy of Doris Dobetsberger (p. 66), Dörthe Saa-
thoff (pp. 5, 62–3, 96–8, 99, 121–7), and personal archives (pp. 129–130, 133). Drawings by Cornelia
Koller.

10 9 8 7 6 5 4 3 2 1

Contents

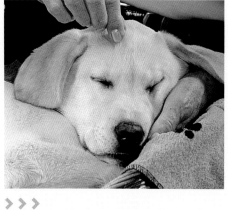

Introduction

Welcome to Puppy School

I'm delighted to introduce my book, *Getting in TTouch with Your Puppy*, produced especially to present the training and concepts of Tellington TTouch Training to puppy owners, breeders, trainers, veterinarians, and vet techs. My intention is to offer you some valuable new tips and techniques for working with young dogs, and it's my hope that the book will enrich your relationship with dogs, as well as your own life.

Perhaps, you've already picked out your new puppy, or maybe you have just begun the search for a young canine companion. My intention in this book is to give you a kind, gentle way to train your puppy to be an ideal companion and well-socialized member of the family.

For those of you who work and care for dogs professionally: you will find effective ideas and methods to aid you in the care of puppies, bitches, and young dogs, and for dealing with challenging behavior, performance, or health issues.

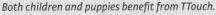

Both children and puppies benefit from TTouch.

My Life with Animals

I was brought up on a farm and was therefore lucky enough to live with animals from the time I was a toddler. When I was three years old, my best friend was a dog, and at nine, I was given my own dog—a Collie named Lassie. Other dogs followed and have been my close companions throughout all the various phases of my life.

I began developing the Tellington Method over 30 years ago. The initial inspiration for the method arose out of my professional work—training and riding horses and teaching career equestrians. In the course of this work, I began to search for successful new teaching methods that would build harmonious communication and cooperation between horse and rider rather than using the commonly accepted methods of force and dominance.

In the 1960s and early 1970s, I co-owned an international, residential "School of Horsemanship," and equine breeding and research center with my first husband, Wentworth Tellington.

In 1974, I closed down my school and set off on a journey around the world that was to change and broaden my life and vision. While traveling, I continued my work in the equestrian world, developing the first training method for horses that combined a form of equine bodywork with classical horsemanship. An essential element of this training is the acknowledgement of each animal as an individual personality. When we recognize each horse as a unique being with individual quirks and strengths, we are able to create a true bond of communication and understanding between horse and human—a relationship of cooperation rather than coercion.

My travels, it turned out, opened my work and life to new dimensions. The practical knowledge I gained over the years meshed with fresh insights. People who cared for animals—whether in a zoo, on a farm, or at home—began hearing of my methods and contacting me. The result was the birth of the Tellington Method.

In 1995, I organized and taught the first three-year certification training for teachers of the Tellington TTouch Training for dogs. Twelve years later, there are more than 1,400 certified Tellington TTouch practitioners teaching in 26 coun-

Learn how to establish a close relationship with your puppy.

tries on five continents. TTouch is practiced in more than 30 countries for horses, dogs, farm animals, and exotics, as well as for humans.

I now live in Hawaii with my husband Roland and our dog Rayne, a West Highland Terrier. When Roland and I are away, traveling the world to present TTouch in seminars, workshops, and expositions, Rayne stays at home, minding the house in the company of a kindly caregiver.

A good relationship between human and dog is founded on trust.

TTouch Training for Puppies

Many of you are the owners of brand new puppies: you have become your dog's trainer, but even more importantly, you are now his family, protector, provider, and companion. Dogs attach closely to humans and to human families, an instinct inherited from their wolf forebears, who lived together in the wild in family groups. Embedded in your puppy's genetic memory is the urge to search for and find a place in your family circle, much as he would have done with his pack in the wild. TTouch is a gentle way to give him the help he needs to feel himself at home.

By using a combination of bodywork (TTouch) and special exercises we call the Playground for Higher Learning (see p. 113), you can train your puppy in ways that will be fun and interesting for him—and for you too. By guiding a young dog through the obstacles and giving five minutes a day of TTouch, you can heighten his ability and willingness to focus and to learn. This method offers you a compassionate and patient means to prepare your pup for the challenges he will meet in life.

Whether you want your puppy for companionship, or you enjoy being active with your dog in programs like agility, dog dancing, obedience, or show, or if you would like to train your puppy to become a therapy dog, TTouch Training will help you lay a foundation for success.

About Tellington TTouch Training

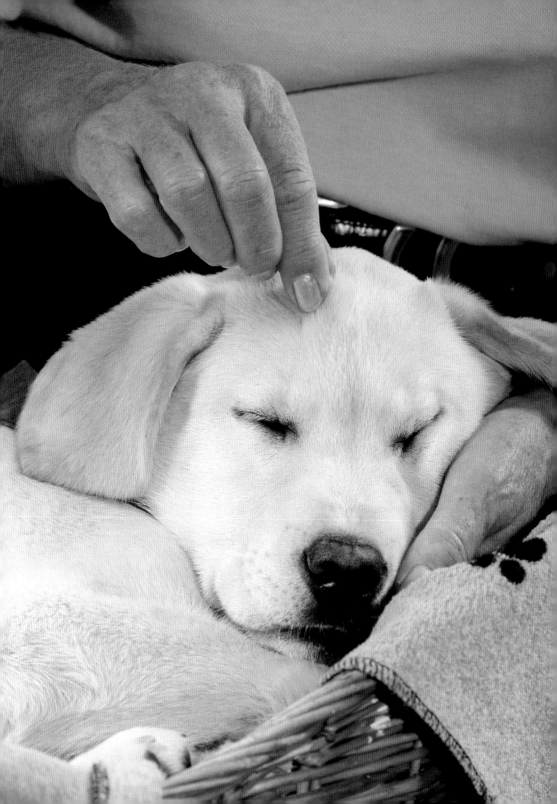

Development of the Tellington TTouch Training Method

The Tellington TTouch Method stems back to the 1970s when I first began developing a new method of training that combined bodywork, ground obstacles, and movement exercises for horses. I originally called it "TEAM"—an acronym for "Tellington Equine Awareness Method." Behind the name are the guiding principles of the method—the concepts of partnership and teamwork, which also embrace the techniques of Tellington TTouch Training. In the ensuing years, it became clear that the Tellington Method was beneficial and effective for many other animals as well. One of the branches that grew from the initial work is Tellington TTouch for dogs, which I began developing in the mid-80s).

The Playground for Higher Learning, or movement exercises, for puppies includes a variety of obstacles. By negotiating his way through them, your puppy will learn to concentrate without stress. Learning becomes enjoyable for both of you.

At first glance, the obstacles seem similar to those used in agility training, but the big difference is that these exercises are performed *slowly*. You can combine

TTouch is lots of fun in a group.

the basic exercises of "Sit" and "Down" as you move through the *Labyrinth* (p. 113). for example, and your puppy will develop mental, physical, and emotional balance that enhances health and well-being. It's also helpful in training your puppy to be a good friend, companion, or family member.

The central component of the Playground for Higher Learning is the *Labyrinth*, an arrangement of six poles placed on flat ground. Puppies learn patience and focus by working together through the *Labyrinth*. You can find more on how to use the exercises for the Playground for Higher Learning on p. 113.

The Body Wrap (p. 87) promotes concentration and a sense of his own body for this boxer.

The Labyrinth (p. 113) is a primary element of Tellington TTouch Training.

Tellington TTouch – The Touch that Builds Trust

Tellington TTouch is an easy-to-learn and gentle form of bodywork that has a positive affect on the behavior, performance, and health of a puppy while also deepening the relationship between puppies and their people. Tellington TTouch, termed "T-Touch" in brief (pronounced "Tee-Touch"), is comprised of circular, lifting, and stroking movements that develop intelligence, confidence, awareness, and trust. The extra "T" in "TTouch" can also be thought of as standing for the "T" in "trust."

Through the warm and gentle contact of the hands in the TTouch method, puppies gain a feeling of special connection and a sense of trust, while learning to enjoy physical contact. For the basic circular TTouch, the skin is pushed gently in a circle-and-a-quarter (see p. 18), inducing a state of simultaneous relaxation and focused awareness. Though one might think of this TTouch as a form of massage, its effect and intention are different from classical massage.

TTouch works on both body and brain in a specific manner—the body becomes relaxed at the same time as the mind's ability to learn and to master new tasks is enhanced. Along with an increased *potential* for learning, the *desire* to learn is also awakened. Animals become better able to overcome instinctive behavior and to master unusual situations with conscious awareness, rather than conditioned reaction. TTouch also helps to support the development of the dog's unique personality.

Tellington TTouch works at the cellular level, enhancing potential for ideal function of the body and mind. Many people who have experienced TTouch report it to be a powerful tool for relieving pain, and overcoming fear and trauma.

Every puppy has a unique personality that can be enhanced with positive training.

We have found this to be also true for dogs of all ages.

The development of the circular TTouch began in the 1980s after 10 years of equine massage and four summers of study with the brilliant Israeli physicist Moshe Feldenkrais at the Humanistic Psychology Institute in San Francisco. With the Feldenkrais Method, I was able to change the behavior of fearful or nervous horses, but it was often a challenge to teach the method to others.

The problem was solved when I discovered the amazingly effective results of

Puppies bring so much joy to people's lives.

TTouch feels good.

gentle circular TTouches, a method that anyone can easily learn. The idea for Tellington TTouch came to me at a magical moment, when a frustrated horse owner asked me for help with her grouchy, touch-resistant mare. "What should I do?" she asked in despair. Quite unexpectedly and spontaneously, I said to her, "Move the skin in a circle." This was not a movement I had ever thought of or used in my work before. She did as I suggested, and the horse immediately relaxed under her hand. I was so surprised and fascinated by the result and the simplicity of the circular movement, that I began

experimenting with different finger and hand positions and pressures, as well as with the direction and timing of a circle.

My sister Robyn helped me in documenting the results, and in giving each TTouch position a name. Over the years, we developed 20 different types of TTouches, but you don't need to know or use them all in order to achieve good results. Even two or three circular, gliding, or lifting TTouches and two to three TTouches on specific areas of the body, are enough to deepen the bond between you and your puppy to help him to "be all he can be."

Beginning on p. 24, you will find explanations of the various TTouches and instructions on how to use them.

TTouch Variations

Tellington TTouches are divided into various categories: *circles, lifts, strokes,* and *specialized TTouches* for application to specific areas of the body. For the *circular* TTouch, the skin is moved in a one-and-a-quarter circle in a clockwise direction. This TTouch employs a number of different hand and finger positions, some of which include the use of the fingertips, the palm, and the back of the hand.

In a *lift,* the skin is gently pushed and then returned to its original position, and in *strokes,* the hands slide over the skin.

The different areas of a puppy's body that employ especially adapted TTouches are the mouth, ears, belly, legs, and tail. Certain TTouches are used to influence the posture of the body or a particular part of the body.

One of the discoveries of the Tellington Method is that altering body posture changes an animal's attitude and behavior without causing stress or fear. We can even observe this connection between body and behavior in ourselves: for instance, when we smile deliberately, we often feel softened and our mood automatically lifts. Take a dog who is anxious, for example—he will express his fear by clamping his tail tightly to his body or between his legs. If you do TTouch bodywork to release and loosen his tail, his anxiety

TTouch is easy to learn.

will be relieved and you'll see a change in his behavior.

Puppies who tend to be aggressive toward other puppies hold their tails in a stiff position. Working on the tail can actually change this behavioral tendency. Of course, the way a dog holds his tail is also attributable to his genetic heritage: some breeds always carry their tails in an upward position (see p. 45).

The Benefits of TTouch

When puppies receive TTouch bodywork, they become eager to learn, which in turn helps them with socialization, maturation, and schooling. For instance, if you intend your puppy to be a sport or therapy dog, TTouch will offer support during the challenging training process, reducing the stress and the strain of new and difficult demands.

A 1985 study conducted in Moscow by Russian veterinarians revealed that horses treated with TTouch demonstrated a remarkable increase in stress-relieving hormones. Over years of working with many thousands of dogs, we have also observed that TTouch dramatically reduces stress in all breeds. Stress reduction is beneficial for all pups, regardless of the role they will be fulfilling later.

Top: The circular Lying Leopard TTouch (p. 28).
Center: Coiled Python TTouch (p. 32).
Bottom: The Tail TTouch (p. 45).

TTouch makes it easier for a puppy to enter the life and environment of a new home and to bond with the members of a new family. The method helps him acclimate to the unfamiliar sounds and sights of a city, and makes learning to ride in a car less stressful for him. Many animal shelters around the world use TTouch to reduce stress in both puppies and adult dogs, because a relaxed, stress-free dog is more appealing and adoptable, and is quicker to establish a relationship with a potential owner.

TTouch is useful in teaching therapy dogs to accept and deal with uncomfortable or unskillful handling when on a visit of compassion to the handicapped or elderly.

The system is also useful in preparing puppies for future training as work, sports, or show dogs, providing them with endurance, self-confidence, and the ability perform well in partnership.

Our experience has shown that circular TTouches activate cells to function at their highest potential for self-healing. Thus, innate healing processes are supported and accelerated, and the body sustains health and vigor.

Beginning with your very first session, you and your puppy will be forming a harmonious relationship and a deep bond.

Preparation for the Mouth TTouch (p. 41).

The puppy will be gaining a sense of trust, self-confidence, strong body awareness, and increased well-being. Using TTouch with your dog also relieves nervousness and tension. Certain TTouches that loosen tight muscles may seem to resemble massage; however, their primary aim is to activate the positive function of the cells and nervous system.

A further positive aspect of the TTouch system is its simplicity: the method is easy to learn and can be practiced virtually anywhere—at home, while traveling, at the veterinarian's office, or in training situations. Even just a few minutes a day can bring about astounding changes and positive results.

This TTouch treatment was so relaxing it ended in a nap.

Basic TTouch Know-How

Using the Circular TTouch

For the basic TTouch circle, the skin is pushed in a circle-and-a-quarter, with just enough pressure to move the skin without sliding across the surface of the hair. How you hold your fingers in executing this circle varies according to the effect you want to achieve. There are, however, certain important points that remain constant: find a comfortable position for yourself; keep the weight of your hand from pressing on the puppy's body; and find the pressure that is agreeable to your dog.

The degree of pressure and the finger position to use will depend on the size and age of your dog: for tiny puppies under three months, you should use only your fingertips—as in the *Raccoon TTouch* (p. 30). Generally, the best TTouches for small, medium, or large breeds under three months old are the *Clouded Leopard* (p. 26), *Lying Leopard* (p. 28), *Raccoon*, and *Tarantulas* (p. 38). The *Hair Slide* (p. 39) is especially appropriate for long-haired breeds. Once puppies in the larger breed categories turn four months or older, some of the other TTouches, like the *Abalone TTouch* (p. 31) are suitable.

One of the most challenging aspects of TTouch is to remember to keep your TTouch light. It helps to imagine that you are "whispering" to the cells with your fingers, developing a nonverbal language of trust. To ensure success, experiment with a variety of TTouches that are comfortable for both you and your puppy.

When working on your puppy, cover the entire body. Make one-and-a-quarter circles, ending each with a one- to two-second pause to allow the message time to register in the brain, then slide across the hair to the next spot (see p. 20). To make sure that you cover the whole body, it's helpful to follow imaginary lines that flow along the puppy's back and sides, from lips, to forehead, to ears, down the legs, onto the foot pads, and over every inch of the tail. Remember to include the underside of the body and the insides of the legs.

The basic TTouch is a circular movement of hand and fingers (see *Clouded Leopard*, p. 26). Imagine a small clock face—approximately $3/4$ inch in diameter—superimposed on the body of the puppy. On the dial, "6 o'clock" is at the base and points toward the ground. Place your fingers on 6 o'clock, and with your fingers softly curved like a paw, push the skin around the clock's face in a clockwise circle. Execute a full circle once around, going past 6 o'clock again to a little beyond, ending between 8 and 9 o'clock.

just a few centimeters away. Making contact with the pads of your four fingers, gently push the skin in a circle and a quarter (as described on p. 18). Hold your wrist up off your arm so there is no contact with the heel of the hand. Allow the joints of your fingers to move flexibly and smoothly. Now, alternatively, try holding your fingers stiffly as you push the skin around.

Pay attention to how it feels. Usually, a stiff finger position will cause you to restrict your breathing, causing tension that will be passed on to the puppy.

TTouch Names

We have given each TTouch an evocative animal name because we found that connecting each TTouch with the characteristics of a particular animal made the

This is how to contain a puppy gently.

Here, pause one to two seconds and then lightly slide across the hair to begin the next circle.

As you circle, maintain a steady pressure and an even speed. It's important that the circles you make are really round and that as you form them your movement is light and flowing.

To find out for yourself how light this TTouch feels, try a little experiment on your arm. Place your thumb lightly on your forearm with the rest of your fingers

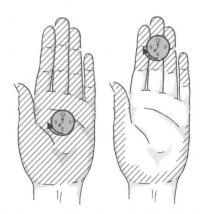

The clock on each hand illustrates the circle-and-a-quarter motion. Left: The Abalone TTouch (p. 31). Right: The Lying Leopard TTouch (p. 28).

movement more fun and easier to learn. I have actually had the honor of working with TTouch on each of the creatures named. For example, the *Clouded Leopard* (p. 26) was inspired by a young female leopard I met in the Los Angeles Zoo. She was born prematurely and had a neurotic reflexive need to knead and suckle. Special circular TTouches for her paws and mouth helped make her aware of what she was doing, and she was able to break the habit.

Timing of Circles

One circle should take between one and three seconds to complete. Nervous dogs often need one-second circles for the first five or six TTouches, until they can benefit from the normal, calming circles of about two seconds. Fast circles are stimulating; slower ones, calming.

The parallel line pattern for making connected circles.

Connecting the TTouches

I usually recommend applying TTouch in lines which run parallel to the spine. The distance between the lines depends on the size of your puppy—the smaller the dog, the closer the lines. After making a two-second TTouch circle, pause for another two seconds to give the message time to register in the brain, then slide across the fur to the next spot.

In some cases you may find it more helpful to begin a session by working on the body with randomly placed circles. This method will act to focus your dog's attention.

Pressure Scale

Since our main goal is to activate cells and neural pathways rather than relax muscles, most of the TTouches are performed with less pressure than you might expect. I have developed a scale in order for you to understand the various pressures ranging from 1 to 10. For puppies, I recommend using a pressure of 1 to 2, while a number 3 pressure is right for young dogs who are older than six months and therefore more muscular.

Try the variations in pressure on yourself. Here's how:

> To feel a number 1 pressure, support your elbow with one hand. Place the thumb of your other hand on your cheekbone, and with your middle

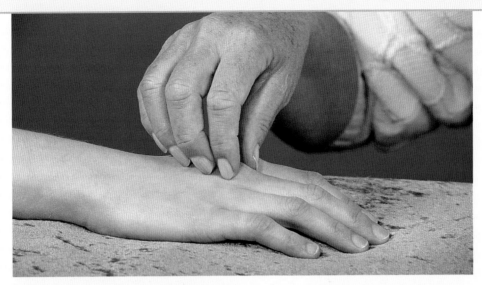

Experiment with TTouch on yourself and on others.

finger slightly curved, push the skin of your closed eyelid in a circle over your eyeball. Make the lightest possible circle without slipping across the skin. Don't use this method if you are wearing contact lenses. Instead, you can also learn the sensation of this TTouch—the lightest one—by circling the delicate skin just under the eye and above the cheekbone. Even if you do not wear contact lenses, it's interesting to try both of these ways. Then, make a circle on your forearm using the same minimal pressure and observe how little indentation you make in the skin.

> To identify a number 3 pressure, circle the skin under the eye and above the cheekbone, only this time, push the skin in a circle with enough pressure that you feel the top of the cheekbone clearly, without pushing hard. Then, retaining the sensory memory of that pressure, make a circle on your forearm and compare this slightly increased pressure to the number 1 pressure.

> To feel a number 6 pressure, repeat the number 3 pressure on your forearm and note the depth of the indentation left on the skin. Now, double the number 3 pressure, and you will be applying a number 6. This is twice as much as I ever recommend for dogs. I use number 6 only for humans—and sometimes horses—who prefer or require a strong pressure.

Observe your dog's reaction to TTouch and adjust the pressure accordingly.

Tips for TTouch Sessions

> Make yourself as comfortable as possible—keep your wrist straight and your fingers flexible, and breathe evenly.

> Clearly visualize the behavior(s) that you wish your puppy to learn.

> Remember your puppy's age. Young dogs are not able to concentrate or hold still over long periods.

> For positive results, keep your sessions short and work with your puppy several times a day. A few minutes a day

Holding a puppy's shoulder and head while he leans into your body gives him a sense of safety and stability.

are enough to help a normal puppy grow into a healthy and well-trained dog.

> To give your dog a sense of safety, hold him in your arms, let him lie in your lap, or have him lean against you.
> Some dogs like to relax and lie down while being TTouched, while others

A restless puppy can be stabilized for a short time by slipping your thumb under his collar to hold him.

feel safer at the beginning if they are sitting or standing. Sometimes, at the beginning of a session, you may have to hold a puppy by the collar to keep him quiet so that you can TTouch every inch of his body.

> To calm a restless puppy, gently stabilize him. Carefully place one hand on his shoulder without exerting pressure. Slip the thumb of the other hand under the dog's collar to hold him.
> For a small puppy you might find it helpful to place him on a soft pad on a tabletop and TTouch him as you sit beside him in a comfortable chair.
> Respond to the reactions of your puppy. If you notice that your dog is reacting negatively, reduce the pressure or tempo, or move to a different area of the body.
> Should you find places where your puppy repeatedly resists contact, have him checked by a veterinarian in case there is something wrong.
> If your puppy is teething, wear gloves and look for the places in his mouth where you can feel new teeth emerging. Teach your puppy to use a chew toy or a knotted rope to satisfy his urge to chew.

Tellington TTouch for Puppies

Circle TTouches

The *circular* Tellington TTouch promotes relaxation and reduces stress and fear. Just a few minutes of TTouch a day is enough to increase a puppy's awareness and ability to learn and cooperate.

The goal of all TTouch bodywork is to stimulate the function and vitality of all the cells in your dog's body in order to keep him happy and healthy for his whole life. To do the circular TTouches, push the skin around in a one-and-a-quarter circle with your fingers or hand (see p. 18).

Clouded Leopard TTouch

Creates good health, releases tension, builds trust

The *Clouded Leopard* is the basic movement for TTouch circles: all the other circular TTouches are variations of it. In performing this TTouch, the slightly curved fingers use only a light pressure. In most cases, the timing for one circle is two seconds, applied with a pressure of 1 to 3.

This TTouch will help your puppy develop confidence and willingness to cooperate. It is especially effective in reducing nervousness and fear. The *Clouded Leopard* is also useful in helping puppies to adapt to new situations, such as a new home or learning to travel in a car.

How-To

Place your slightly curved hand on your

Clouded Leopard TTouches on the head create trust.

The fingers move the skin very gently and lightly, and there is no pressure from the weight of the hand.

puppy's body. Keeping your fingers close together, move the skin around in a one-and-a-quarter circle.

As shown in the drawing, the shaded areas of the fingers should make contact with the dog's hair. The thumb rests on the puppy's body, but makes only a very light connection.

Keep your joints flexible, so that your fingers, hand, arm, and shoulders can move with ease. Your other hand should rest lightly on the puppy's body, gently stabilizing him.

Envisioning the face of a clock (see p. 19), start at 6 o'clock and push the skin in a clockwise circle back around to 6 o'clock, and then a bit further, till you arrive between 8 and 9 o'clock. Pause here for one to two seconds.

As soon as you have finished one circle, connect it to the next by lightly sliding along the hair to the next spot (see p. 20).

The Clouded Leopard TTouch. The blue hatch marks on the fingertips indicate the points of contact.

The Lying Leopard TTouch is used to foster relaxation.

Lying Leopard TTouch

For relaxation and deepening your relationship with your puppy

In the *Lying Leopard TTouch*, the soft contact of the flattened hand brings warmth and relaxation. The hand places no weight on the body, and the fingers make a connection with light circles. This gentle TTouch deepens the bond of trust between you and your dog.

This TTouch usually uses a number 1 or 2 pressure with each circle lasting two seconds.

The *Lying Leopard* is one of the basic TTouches used to foster relaxation.

How-To

Place your flattened hand softly on the dog's body and move the skin around in a one-and-a-quarter circle with your fingers. The shaded areas in the drawing illustrate where the contact is usually made. In some cases—for example, when working on the legs or head—you should not place the heel of your hand on the dog's body, because you will not be able to hold your wrist in a relaxed, and yet straight position.

Picture the face of a clock (see illustration) and starting at 6 o'clock, push the skin around in a clockwise circle, passing 6 o'clock again until you arrive between 8 and 9 o'clock. After a pause of one to two seconds, slide across the hair to the next position.

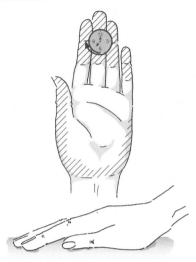

Lying Leopard circles on the mouth are effective for building trust.

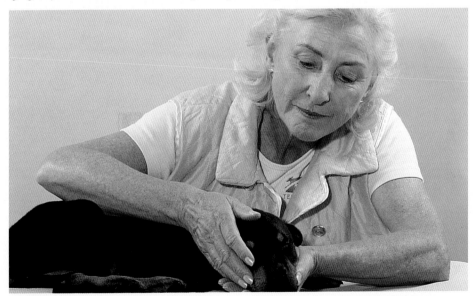

How-To

Bend the tips of your fingers at a 90-degree angle and move the skin in a tiny one-and-a-quarter circle. Remember, this TTouch is done with a very light pressure. Usually, the thumb will have no, or at most, a very light contact with the body.

In order to keep the contact light and flowing, the palm of the hand does not make contact. The other hand is placed comfortingly on the dog's body, giving him a sense of stability and safety.

Raccoon TTouch

For mouth, paws, and small areas of the body

The *Raccoon TTouch* is ideal for working on the mouth, lips, and paws, as well as on the bodies of small puppies. This TTouch is also helpful when you need to address areas like scar tissue or places that are burning, sensitive, painful, or itchy. The *Raccoon TTouch* relieves these ailments in a short time. Moreover, with this TTouch you can speed up the healing process in the affected part of the body.

Make the circles as small and with as little pressure as possible—that is to say a number 1 or 2. The usual timing to complete a one-and-a-quarter circle is two seconds.

In the Raccoon TTouch, only the fingertips move the skin.

Abalone TTouch

For sensitive, fearful, and sick puppies

The *Abalone TTouch* is perfect for sensitive, shy, or large puppies because the completely flattened hand imparts warmth

The Abalone TTouch imparts a sense of calm, security, and safety.

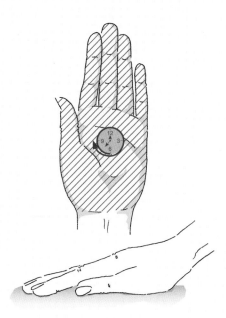

In the Abalone TTouch, the whole hand moves the skin.

and security. This TTouch is also useful to calm and relax a nervous animal. It helps overcome fear and resistance in puppies who are sensitive to touch or to being brushed. Normally, the pressure used is a number 1 to 2 with a two-second TTouch circle.

How-To

Place your flattened hand, palm side down, on the dog's body so that you make total contact. Your entire hand is used to push the skin around in the usual one-and-a-quarter circle.

The Coiled Python TTouch works to increase awareness and the feeling of security and confidence.

Coiled Python TTouch (aka the Combined TTouch)

Promotes focused awareness

This TTouch, a combination of a circular TTouch and the *Python TTouch* (p. 34), is a very useful way to promote awareness. The circular movement prompts response, while the connected Python TTouch deepens the breath and relaxes the body. The *Coiled Python TTouch* is a valuable TTouch for your first sessions. In these early sessions, you might want to accustom the puppy to being TTouched by using a soft glove or a piece of sheepskin.

How-To

After completing a TTouch circle, for instance a *Lying Leopard TTouch* (p. 28), go to

The Lying Leopard TTouch plus the Python TTouch.

9 o'clock on your imaginary clock face and push the skin up vertically. Pause there for a moment and then release and return to 9 o'clock again.

Llama TTouch

For insecure and timid puppies

The *Llama TTouch* is done with the backs of the fingers. Sensitive and fearful puppies perceive this TTouch as less threatening than others. Also, it is a practical TTouch for people whose fingers are somewhat stiff. The *Llama TTouch* is an excellent method for accustoming young puppies to being handled. It also works as a way to instill trust so that you can easily move on to other TTouches. The pressure is a number 1 to 2, and each TTouch should last two seconds.

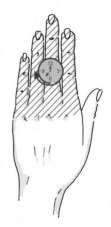

How-To

For the *Llama TTouch*, use the backs of your fingers to make the one-and-a-quarter circle. Begin, as usual, at 6 o'clock on your imaginary clock face (see above), pushing the skin around in a one-and-a-quarter circle, and gliding across the hair to the spot for your next circle.

The Llama TTouch is perfect for sensitive or fearful puppies.

Stroking and Lifting TTouches

In the *stroking* or *lifting* TTouches, one or both hands move across the dog's hair. These TTouches activate your puppy's circulation and awaken awareness in his entire body. Such TTouches also serve to relax the dog and to regulate his breathing. They promote trust between puppy and human and are a friendly, gentle way to establish contact.

Python TTouch

Stimulates circulation, promotes relaxation, awakens body awareness

The *Python TTouch* is especially suited for promoting relaxation, awakening body awareness and improving circulation. Using this TTouch on your puppy's legs aids circulation and promotes self-confidence. You will also improve mobility and balance. The pressure is from a number 1 to a number 2.

When the *Python TTouch* is used in combination with circular TTouches, it is called the *Coiled Python TTouch* and works to enhance awareness (see p. 32).

How-To

When working with this TTouch, place your entire flattened hand on the body and gently and slowly move the skin upward. On the legs, use your fingers to lift

Python TTouches down the right leg.

as much skin as you are able to hold. At the top of the lift movement, pause for a few seconds, and then slowly move the skin back down to the point where you began the lift.

Maintain the same contact and pressure throughout the entire movement. If your puppy is feeling very frisky, pause at the top of the lift a bit longer and take double the time in the downward movement than you did on the upward one. This will deepen the relaxing effect of the TTouch.

When working on the puppy's legs, slide down a finger width after each lift,

Stroking and Lifting TTouches

and continue in this way until you reach the paws.

When working on the body, perform the Python TTouches in equal distances and in parallel lines.

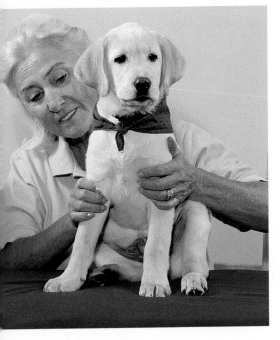

Dogs enjoy this TTouch especially because it is performed across or against the lay of the hair. You can improve your dog's sense of well-being by stroking over various areas of the body, for example from the belly to the back, or across the shoulders.

How-To

Start at the belly, spread and curve your fingers slightly. With your fingertips, lightly slide upward through the fur and onto the back. Your fingers should be relaxed, making the movement as light and flowing as possible.

After the first stroke, move your hand about a hand's width along the belly toward the hind legs. Then move on to the thigh and up across the pelvis. The distance between the strokes depends on the size of the dog. Continue in this way over the whole body.

You can improve your puppy's sense of well-being by performing Lick of the Cow's Tongue from the belly to the back.

Lick of the Cow's Tongue
Increases body awareness
The *Lick of the Cow's Tongue* is a long, diagonal stroke across the dog's body. It relaxes, stimulates circulation, and increases an animal's sense of his own body.

Lick of the Cow's Tongue stroke.

Noah's March
Used to begin and close a TTouch session

Noah's March is the TTouch you use to begin and close a TTouch session. You can also use these long, calming strokes, performed along the lay of the hair, to acquaint yourself with a new puppy or dog. We often end a TTouch session with *Noah's March* because the sweeping strokes along the entire body connect and integrate all the areas that have been worked on. (If you are only going to TTouch your puppy for a few minutes, it is not necessary to start and end with *Noah's March*.)

How-To

With your flattened hand, softly follow the contours of the body. Keep your fingers relaxed and sensitive as you stroke. Before you begin work with a new puppy, establish contact with several calm, slow, and short *Noah's March* TTouches. For the first meeting, I often use the *Llama TTouch*,

The Noah's March stroke.

or a sheepskin glove for *Noah's March*.

When you are working with a new dog who is timid or shy, or who has had bad experiences, make your first approach from the side rather than directly from the front. If the puppy does allow you to approach from the front, turn your head away and your body sideways. Talk to him in a calm, soft voice, soften your gaze, and lean your body slightly forward. Invite the puppy to come to you. Your body language will have a calming effect on him, engendering confidence.

When first handling a new puppy, you can establish contact
with a sheepskin glove and Noah's March.

Your puppy will love your fingers "walking" from his hips to his head in Tarantulas Pulling the Plow.

Tarantulas Pulling the Plow

Sensitizes, promotes circulation, feels pleasurable

This TTouch is a lighter, modified version of an ancient Mongolian form of bodywork called *chua'ka*, used to release fear before battle. It reduces over-sensitivity to contact, boosts circulation and is helpful for dogs who have limited body awareness. With this TTouch, you can also increase your puppy's trust in you. After your puppy has become familiar with *Tarantulas Pulling the Plow*, he will love receiving it. It's a good choice for sharing a few pleasurable moments. You'll find that you have become relaxed right along with your puppy.

How-To

Gently place your hands side by side on the puppy's body. Your fingertips should point forward in the direction of the movement. Your thumbs should angle away from the hands and toward each other, and the tips can touch lightly. Now, use both index fingers to simultaneously take a "step"—about 1½ inches—forward, allowing the thumbs to drag along behind like a plow. The skin in front of your thumbs will be gently rolled. Next, take a simultaneous step with your two middle fingers. In this way your index and middle fingers "walk," making alternate steps while your thumbs are pulled along behind. The entire motion is performed in an even and smooth manner.

Your index and middle fingers "walk" in this TTouch, pulling your thumbs along behind.

In "walking" along your dog's back from the hips to the head, do not stroke over the spine, but on either side. For a small puppy you can walk the fingers of one hand rather than two, dragging the single thumb behind.

Hair Slides

Relaxes and prepares for brushing and trimming

Doing *Hair Slides* is an excellent way of building a relationship with your dog, as these TTouches are wonderfully relaxing for both of you. *Hair Slides* are a pleasant experience and are therefore a good way to prepare puppies for brushing and grooming.

How-To

Take up a small tuft of hair between your fingers at an angle of about 90 degrees and as close to the roots of the hair as possible. Follow the lay of the fur and slowly slide upward to the tips of the hair. For long-haired dogs, use the spaces between the fingers of your flattened hand to take up more of the hair, and softly slide upward. Or, you can grasp the hair between thumb and forefinger as close to the roots as possible, make a one-and-a-quarter TTouch circle, and then slide softly and slowly up along the hair to the tips.

If you perform your *Hair Slides* slowly and gently, you'll discover that this TTouch is not only calming and enjoyable for your puppy, but for you, as well.

Hair Slides are pleasurable and relaxing for both puppy and human.

Inchworm
Works to reduce sensitivity and tension

The *Inchworm* reminds me of the movements of an inchworm going forward, hence the name. This TTouch is helpful for puppies who are sensitive and nervous, who don't like being picked up, or who are fearful of strangers. The *Inchworm* can also help to release tension in the shoulders and back by relaxing these areas.

How-To

Lightly place both your hands on your puppy's back about 1/4 inch apart. Both hands then slowly and simultaneously push toward each other, folding the skin between them gently inward. Use only enough pressure to perform the movement. Pause briefly, and then allow the skin to return to where you began the movement, but take twice as long to release the skin as you did for pushing it together because this is the motion that lets go of tension.

Repeat this TTouch on various areas of the body, remembering to keep your hands soft and light and to synchronize the movement with your own breathing.

First, the hands are softly pushed toward each other (top), then they move back to return to the original position (bottom).

TTouches for Parts of the Body

These TTouches are meant for special work on specific areas of the body, for instance the ears, the tail, or the legs. These specialized TTouches utilize *circular* or *stroking* techniques and can alter physical conditions, behavior, and attitude. The *Ear TTouch*, for example, has a calming effect and is helpful in cases of shock and injury. The *Tail* and *Mouth TTouches* influence the emotions and change behavior patterns. The *Belly Lift* relieves stress and colic and has a positive effect on respiration.

Mouth TTouch

Influences emotions

TTouch on and in the mouth activates the limbic system—the part of the brain that controls emotion and underlies the learning process. Though *Mouth TTouches* always support health, they are especially effective for puppies who suffer from fear, stress, nervousness, hyperactivity, or uncontrolled barking and whimpering. As amazing as it sounds, many dogs who snap, bite, or are aggressive toward other dogs respond particularly positively to the *Mouth TTouch* and are able to change their behavior.

This TTouch also encourages healthy gums, and the enhanced circulation re-

The Lying Leopard TTouch (p. 28) on the muzzle and the gums while the other hand gently supports the head.

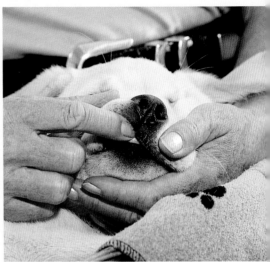

Tiny Raccoon TTouches (p. 30) on the gums using the first and middle fingers. The other hand gently supports the puppy's mouth under the chin.

duces teething difficulties. When puppies are teething, they often have the urge to chew on things, and *Mouth TTouches* relieve some of the discomfort they experience. *Mouth TTouches* are excellent preparation for examinations by the vet and handling by a judge at a dog show.

How-To

Begin with *Lying Leopard TTouches* (p. 28) on the outside of the muzzle. Use your other hand to support your puppy's head.

Slide one or two of your fingers, depending on the size of the puppy, under the lips along the gums, using gentle *Lying Leopard TTouches* to cover every inch. *Raccoon TTouches* (p. 30) on the gums

ease teething problems and help keep the gums healthy.

Dampening your fingers in lukewarm water can facilitate moving them along the gums.

Ear TTouch
Calms, relieves pain, aids in emergencies

The *Ear TTouch* is one of the most important TTouches in the Tellington Method. It has been known for many centuries that working on the ears of humans has a positive effect on the entire body and each of its organs, and to this day, acupuncturists treat patients by working on the ears.

The *Ear TTouch* is especially important

in cases of shock, when circulation may be breaking down. Doing *Ear TTouches* immediately after an accident, or before and after surgery, stabilizes the circulation and can even save lives.

The *Ear TTouch* can also be used effectively to relieve pain and to calm hyperactive dogs. Puppies who have been "treated" to the *Ear TTouch* will often come to their owners to request a repeat performance.

How-To

Facing in the same direction as your puppy, stabilize the dog's head with one hand. Grasp the opposite ear between the thumb and fingers of your other hand in such a way that the thumb is on top. Gently stroke the ear from the middle of the head all the way down the ear to the tip.

Work different areas of the ear with each stroke so that you cover every square inch. Do not pull the ear, but just slide softly over the hair.

Stroke floppy ears out to the side, supporting the ear with your hand. If your dog has upright ears, stroke upward from the base. When you are ready to switch to the opposite ear, change hands.

If you are trying to help a dog that is in pain or in shock, you may want to make your strokes faster and apply slightly more pressure. To help your dog relax, use slow and gentle slides.

Circular TTouches (p. 26) on the underside of the ear.

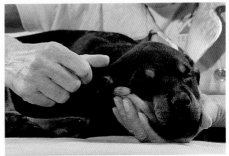

Stroking the ear.

Belly Lift with one hand on the rib cage.

The opposite hand rests on the back to stabilize the dog.

Belly Lift using an elastic bandage.

Belly Lift

Reduces stress, aids in digestion, relaxes

Belly Lifts relax a dog's stomach muscles and deepen breathing, thus relieving cramps. The technique is particularly effective for digestive problems and nervousness. It is also very beneficial for pregnant females.

Belly Lifts can be accomplished in numerous ways: either with one or both hands, or with a cloth or an elastic bandage. Whatever method you choose, the important thing is to go slowly and maintain a light contact.

How-To

Place one hand on the dog's back (for stabilization) and the other under the belly (you can also use an elastic bandage as pictured in the photograph). Quietly and over a period of six seconds, lift the hand under the belly upward and hold in place for approximately six more seconds. Then very slowly (taking about 10 seconds) release the contact. The release is the most important and effective aspect of the *Belly Lift*.

To relax your puppy, begin at the rib cage and move back in increments of one hand's breadth until you reach the hind legs. If the puppy proves sensitive, begin where the rib cage ends.

A gentle tail pull.

Circling the tail in both directions.

Tail TTouch
Reduces fear and aggression

Tail TTouch can help your puppy to overcome fear, timidity, insecurity, aggression, and fear of loud noises. Small, gentle circles and very soft tail pulls can bring improvement for hip dysplasia.

Of course, different breeds boast different types of tails, but for all breeds, a dog's posture and the way he moves and carries his tail will indicate his attitude. When a dog is wagging his tail in an easygoing manner, he is demonstrating joy and good humor. However, a nervous, hyperactive, or insecure dog may wag his tail constantly and very fast. This is often not understood to be the expression of a problem. I believe such nervous tail action is due to insecurity, a state which can be effectively altered through TTouch.

Circle TTouches (p. 26) on every inch of the tail.

A clamped tail expresses fear and submission, a tail held stiff and high points to aggression and dominance. However, no

Careful Tail Pulls increase body awareness: the left hand supports the shoulder while the right hand works the tail.

matter how your puppy is holding his tail, if you can get him to relax it, you'll be able to influence his attitude.

How-To

Prelude

A good way to begin working with the *Tail TTouch* is to start by using such TTouches as the *Raccoon* (p. 30) or *Clouded Leopard* (p. 26). Begin at the root of the tail and make connected TTouches to the tip. Be sure to include the underside of the tail.

Circling the Tail

Using one hand, lightly grasp the tail near the root. Holding the tail between the thumb and forefinger, carefully rotate it in both directions. Alternate directions after each single rotation, going clockwise and counterclockwise.

Tail Pull

Hold the tail at the root with one hand. Pull gently and evenly, pause briefly, and slowly release.

Paw TTouch

Prepares for nail clipping and promotes balance

The *Paw TTouch* helps prepare puppies for toenail clipping, a potential challenge throughout a dog's life. It's also helpful for dogs who are timid or insecure because

TTouches for Parts of the Body

they tend not to have a good physical awareness of their legs. The *Paw TTouch* is useful, too, for dogs who become uneasy when faced with walking on smooth or slippery surfaces. TTouch treatment has a positive effect on a puppy's stability, thereby also strengthening emotional and mental balance.

Working between the paw pads.

How-To

For this TTouch, your puppy can stand, sit, or lie down. In order to relax him, first do some of the TTouches he enjoys most. Then, starting at the top of the leg, do *Clouded Leopard TTouches* (p. 26) all the way down to the paw. Do gentle *Raccoon TTouches* (p. 30) on the paw and pads, making sure to cover the whole area. If your dog is ticklish between the pads, work with slightly more pressure in these areas. Ticklishness may be caused by long hair between the pads, and if this is the case with your dog, I recommend trimming it.

Paw TTouch improves both physical and mental balance.

Raising Puppies with the Tellington TTouch Method

The Fundamentals of Early Education

In practicing the Tellington Method with puppies I make the following two promises that I hope will mean as much to you as they do to me:

1. The golden rule for puppies: Treat your puppy as you would like to be treated.
2. When working with puppies, I will treat them in a loving and respectful way, while simultaneously setting boundaries. In this manner, a puppy will respect me and learn to behave in ways that are appropriate for him as a member of the family.

Now I am ready to begin the puppy's education with patience and compassion.

TTouch develops a puppy's wish to learn, so that exercises like "Sit," "Down," and "Come" are easily understood. Then the educational process can always be a positive experience free of stress or pressure for both puppy and person. In fact, working with your dog can actually promote your own health. Studies have shown that people who live with animals are healthier and feel more fulfilled. For example, it's been demonstrated that living with a pet lowers a person's blood pressure and stress levels.

Friendship and trust are important in educating your puppy.

"Stay" indicated with clear body language.

Praise and acknowledgement for a job well done make learning easy.

Communication without Pressure

When I teach a dog, I always consider the personality, behavior, and learning ability of each individual animal. I advance step by step, showing the dog exactly what I expect of him.

Understanding an animal's behavior enables one to react in a respectful, intelligent, and friendly manner. I believe there is always a reason for any type of behavior. Aggression comes from fear, pain, or insecurity, so I always look for these underlying causes of unwanted behavior in order to help an animal.

Clear communication and positive reinforcement are powerful ingredients in teaching him to understand what is right. Consequently, the Tellington Method works without using techniques that ignore the dog's personality and demand submission. Punishment, in my opinion, is superfluous, only creating stress and bad feeling. Both of these methods prevent or impair learning.

My training method for a puppy is based on communicating to him, in a friendly and clear way, *exactly* what I want from him. Speaking to him quietly in an encouraging and warm tone furthers learning. You'll find that speaking in this way also has a remarkable effect on your own stress level. (For some amazing insights on the subject, I recommend the book *The Healing Power of Water* by Masaru Emoto, which demonstrates how words and tone play a role in our every-day life (see further discussion below).

First, I speak to the dog using his name, talking to him in a respectful, friendly, and inviting way. I match my tone of voice to what the situation calls for: If I want to stimulate the dog, I speak to him in a lively and encouraging tone. If I want to handle, calm him, or ask him to sit or lie down, my tone becomes soft and low. In general, pitching the voice higher is effective because to a puppy's ear, it sounds positive. With Tellington TTouch Training, we don't speak in "commando" style because such a manner creates tension—not only in dogs, but in humans, too. It's a common belief that we have to dominate our animals. Actually, such an approach creates a stressful atmosphere in which neither dog nor human is happy.

Immediately after a puppy has done something well, I confirm his behavior with words of praise—"Thank you," "Very good," or other words that offer positive feedback. Here, too, tone of voice is important: using tone as well as words, I express my pleasure at the puppy's accomplishment. I've found that exaggerating my delight works really well.

It makes a great difference whether I formulate a request in a demanding "Do it!" way, or in a friendly "Let's do this." fashion. The end result is very different—whether the communication is interspe-

Attentive puppies make good students.

cies or between humans. Dogs are intelligent and social souls, perfectly capable of understanding and interpreting the meaning behind words and tone of voice. Experience has shown me that friendliness and respect bring much better results than dominance. There is much to be said for treating a dog with consideration, because he will then behave considerately in return.

The Japanese scholar Masaru Emoto (mentioned previously) has conducted exhaustive experiments about the nature and formation of ice crystals. He discovered that while different temperatures affect the form the crystal takes, so does the degree of dirt in the water. In the course of his research, he also found that moods could be transferred through water: ice crystals that formed when orders like, "Do it!" were sent out actually developed inharmonious shapes. However, when the input was an encouraging "Let's do it," exactly the opposite occurred—the crystals developed into symmetrical and beautiful forms.

For me, this is further proof that when training a puppy, a respectful and attentive attitude is very important.

Tips for Choosing a Puppy

Consider your situation honestly. How much space, time, and help can you give a new canine companion? If you don't have much time to walk, educate, and play with your dog, you should get a breed that will accommodate these conditions—for instance, a small, calm dog. If you prefer larger dogs, look for a breed that is known to have an even temperament, such as a greyhound. Another possibility is to find a responsible person to help with the daily care or regular walking schedule for your puppy.

All working dogs, like herding or hunting dogs, were initially bred to perform a job. It's important to realize that such breeds need tasks that approximate their

Am I the right dog for you?

Mixed breeds make wonderful companions.

original purpose, or in many cases, problems will arise.

Over the centuries, certain characteristics inherent in each breed were sought out and heightened according to the purpose and tasks the dogs were to perform. Roughly, these tasks are herding, guarding, hunting, and companioning. The latter category includes many lapdogs, who over time have been bred simply to look beautiful and be good company. Which category is right for you?

There are numerous informative books on the characteristics of the different breeds, which can help you to find the answer. When you have decided on the breed and are ready to pick out your puppy, please take good care to check the reputation of the kennel and breeder. Ask for references from other clients who have bought puppies there. Be on guard against unscrupulous breeders who run "puppy mills," places that turn out too many puppies, some of whom may actually be sick, overbred, or provided with false papers.

Of course, you may not want to go through a breeder or kennel to get your puppy. Many people find a new "best friend" in an animal shelter, where mixed breeds, purebreds, and older dogs are all waiting for just the right human to take them home.

Calming Signals

Dogs communicate with each other in many ways, signaling with their bodies, eyes, tails, and facial expressions in a manner that can speak volumes. They use calming and pacifying signals as a way to establish hierarchy and to avoid conflict. The Norwegian dog trainer Turid Rugaas lists these movements in her book *On Talking Terms with Dogs* as: turning the head and body aside; turning the backside to the other dog; licking the nose or lips; blinking the eyes; walking slowly; sitting down; yawning; or sniffing the ground (see p. 131).

We humans can also use body language as a way to communicate with canines. To approach a dog who is unfamiliar to you, come toward him from the side, look away while also softening your gaze, and blink. This is the way well-socialized dogs greet each other.

Your puppy needs contact with other pups in order to learn to "speak" and to understand the language of these many signals. Dogs with black faces for instance, will indicate a calming intention by using licking more than other signals, because their facial expressions are more difficult to interpret. Long hair falling over the eyes also makes communication between dogs harder.

A trusting first encounter.

First Encounter

From the first time you go to a shelter or a breeder to choose a puppy, the Tellington TTouch can help you to build a relationship with the dogs you meet.

If the puppies are newborn or very young, you'll be visiting a number of times, because these little ones usually need to stay with their mother for 8 to 12 weeks. They need this period to be nourished by their mother's milk and by the cozy warmth and nest-like closeness and security provided by "Mom" and siblings. In these weeks, too, they learn important rules and lessons in socialization by relating to each other.

It's helpful to use this time to observe the mother and her young ones. How do the puppies behave? How does the mother's behavior toward them change as they mature? What toys do they prefer? What are their living quarters like? Your observations will give you important feedback about the quality of the breeder and the character of the puppies. For example, you may see that certain puppies cower in a corner and don't communicate with you; others may seem nervous, shy, or weak.

Should such a puppy win your heart, TTouch can be very useful in helping him to overcome his difficulties. However, such behaviors or appearances should not be dismissed, as they can be indications of sickness, and it's advisable to have the puppy checked by a vet before bringing him home.

If you feel that the mother and her puppies are not behaving normally or that they are not being properly cared for, you should seek another breeder.

Mother and puppy learn TTouch together.

Once you have decided on a particular puppy and have the permission of the breeder or shelter to visit, use TTouch to establish a connection with him so that he feels trust in you and will be less stressed when entering his new home.

> Begin with *circular* TTouches on the body: the *Lying Leopard* (p. 28), *Llama* (p. 33), or *Raccoon TTouches* (p. 30) are appropriate, or if the puppy is very small, just tiny *Raccoon TTouches*.

> Make very careful *Ear TTouches* (p. 42).

> Go slowly over the whole body with *Noah's March* (p. 37).

A few moments are all you need to establish contact. Play with your puppy if he is interested.

Many puppies are very homesick when they are first separated from their mother and siblings. With TTouch, you can establish a bond between you and your puppy that alleviates or shortens this difficult period.

Naming Your Puppy

A short note about names and their meanings: if you are giving your pup a new name, make sure that it sounds pleasant and that the meaning of the name is positive. I've often seen cases

>TTOUCH TIP

Lying Leopard TTouch, p. 28
Llama TTouch, p. 33
Raccoon TTouch, p. 30
Ear TTouch, p. 42
Noah's March, p. 37

rest easy that he will not relieve himself in the house when you are gone, or chew on your rugs, furniture, and other valued items. The crate also makes an excellent place for your dog to hang out when you have company.

where the behavior and character of dogs will match the names they have been given, both in positive as well as negative ways. Names like "Sunny" or "Lucky"— names that sound good to the ear and suit the animal—create a good feeling in both human and dog.

Crate Training

Teaching your puppy to feel safe and secure in a crate is a valuable tool for establishing successful behavior. As he becomes accustomed to the crate, he will begin to experience this special place as his own personal domain, and you will have established a base that will prove useful for many other aspects of training.

Dogs often like to lie under a chair because they are den animals by nature. Therefore, when properly introduced to a crate, they will love its protective feeling. A crate for your dog offers benefits for your own life as well: with your dog happily ensconced in his crate, you can

TTouch helps accustom puppies to new quarters.

What You Will Need

Crates are available in plastic, metal, or nylon. I prefer a crate with a removable top, because it allows you to TTouch your dog while he's in it. But more important than choosing the type of crate is making sure that you pick one that is the right size. Dogs instinctively keep their dens clean. However, if you give your dog a crate that's too big, he'll have enough room to create a spot away from his sleeping area to relieve himself. If the crate is too small, he will be uncomfortable. Pick a crate in which the dog can stand up, lie down comfortably, and turn around with ease. If your puppy is a breed that will grow large, get him a big crate and temporarily reduce the space by blocking off a section of the interior with a divider panel or another safe, immovable method.

Place the crate in an area where your family spends time together to keep your puppy from feeling lonely or punished while he's in his "house."

During the initial training phase, it's safer not to place bedding or soft toys inside the crate, because these items can encourage frenetic play and lead to accidents. Once your dog is reliably housetrained and comfortable in his crate, you can then add bedding.

Make sure, too, that you have plenty of very small, delicious treats on hand—for

Step-by-step, the puppy learns to trust his crate.

instance, bits of chicken, cheese, sausage, or liver. A Kong® filled with treats will give your puppy something to work on in his crate when he's not sleeping or resting.

Use your hands to guide the puppy backward into the crate.

Teaching Your Puppy to Enjoy the Crate

Once your dog is familiar with his crate, he'll adopt it as his new home and will enjoy spending time in it. To get your dog acquainted with the crate, place a few treats inside for him to retrieve. If he hesitates, place a few just inside the crate door to encourage him to come closer. The moment he enters the crate, praise him and immediately reward him with another treat. Gradually toss the treat a little further back into the crate to get your dog used to entering and exiting. Don't close the door—you just want him to get used to going in and out. Every time he walks in, say a word like "Bedtime." Your dog will soon understand what the word means and learn to go in on his own when he hears it.

As soon as your puppy seems comfortable walking in and out of the crate, go ahead and start closing the door behind him for a few seconds. While he's inside, keep praising him. It's helpful to give him a toy or Kong® to play with. When he's being quiet, tell him he is "Such a good dog!"

Continue practicing with treats and toys while gradually increasing the time spent in the crate with the door closed. Remember, practice makes perfect. Once your dog is fully house-trained you can give him a choice of sleeping in or out of the crate.

Riding in the Car

If you want travel in a car to be as stress-free as possible for your dog, make sure that before taking him on his first trip, he is already happy and secure with you and his new home. Some dogs get nauseous or become nervous in a car. In that case, you can use TTouch on the whole body to strengthen his emotional, mental, and physical balance. *Ear TTouch* (p. 42)

Repeatedly guiding a puppy into a topless crate works wonders.

>TTOUCH TIP

Ear TTouch, p. 42
Mouth TTouch, p. 41
Lying Leopard TTouch, p. 28
Python TTouch, p. 34
Paw TTouch, p. 46
Body Wrap, p. 87

can overcome nausea. *Python TTouches* (p. 34) on all four legs, from his elbows or knees to his paws, create good inner balance. Applying the *Body Wrap* (p. 87) or *T-Shirt* (p. 88) can calm a dog who is restive in a car.

Some dogs immediately fall in love with car travel. Others can be fearful, while still others can become carsick. To help prepare your puppy for travel, use TTouches to enhance self-confidence and stress resistance.

The First Drive Home

The first day you bring your puppy to his new home, he'll be experiencing a disorienting world of unfamiliar faces, sounds, smells, and sights, starting with the car trip to your house or apartment. If you're taking him home in a car, you can do a lot to reduce the puppy's stress level by preparing him for the ride beforehand. The first step is to teach him to enter his

TTouch in the crate gives your puppy a sense of security.

transport crate and feel comfortable inside it. Then, if it is possible, take him for a short practice drive in a car and experiment with various TTouches to see which ones he finds most relaxing.

On the "big day," see if you can find someone willing to drive the two of you home. Sit in the backseat and hold the puppy in your lap or place him on a soft cushion beside you. Should your puppy be large and active, keep him in his traveling crate on the backseat next to you, where you can reassure and calm him.

If the trip is a long one, plan on making frequent stops. When you take him out of the car, make sure he is on a leash.

>LINDA'S TIP

If possible, before you take your puppy home, sit with him in a parked car for a few short sessions. Once he feels at ease there, put him in his crate with a nice soft pad or blanket. Place the crate safely on the floor of the car and then slowly drive around the block. This helps to accustom the puppy to motion. You can find further useful information and tips on travel safety if you search the Internet for "safe travel with dogs."

Preparing Your Home

Since your puppy will be a companion who shares your living space with you, it's important to make your home as dog-friendly as possible.

Sleeping Area

Establish the puppy's crate as his bed and sleeping area, right from his first day and night at home. It would be ideal to accustom him to the crate before you bring him home (see p. 57). When he is still young, the crate should be his personal "house"; his place for rest and retreat, as well as for sleep (see p. 69). It can also serve as a familiar, comfortable, and safe container for car travel. When the dog is older, he can graduate to a comfy blanket or a special dog bed for rest and sleep. Place the bed in a quiet and sheltered area of your home.

Carrier Crates

There are many types of crates for sale, and they come in all different sizes and shapes. Be sure to pick the appropriate size for your puppy (see p. 58). To help your dog feel more at home in his crate, furnish it with a cushion and a stuffed animal or chew-rope that bear the scent of his mother and siblings.

If You Have a Yard

If you are lucky enough to have a yard, reserve a space where your puppy can play. The area should be enclosed by a safety fence to keep the dog from running away and to limit his territory.

Toys

There are myriads of toys available for puppies and dogs, but not many are worth mentioning. My favorites are rope chews and Kongs® (hollow rubber toys that you can fill with food or treats). Give your puppy a Kong® stuffed with his favorite snack, and your furniture and

A friend helps make the crate inviting.

The red ball is a Kong®, a useful toy for puppies.

slippers will be spared his enthusiastic teething attentions.

How and Where to Feed

Place your dog's food and water dishes in a permanent location. The spot should be accessible, but not in a hallway. Make sure that the bowls can't slide around on the floor. Because I recommend rewarding your dog with food, I suggest that you keep a stock of delicious (to him) treats on hand. Measure the number of treats against the amount of his daily meals, so that you don't overfeed him. Offer him only very small treats so that he can chew them without a problem.

Nutrition for Puppies
by Dr. Martina Simmerer
Veterinary practitioner in chiropractic, acupuncture, homeopathy, and TTEAM

When Linda asked me to write a few lines about nutrition for young dogs, my first thought was, "That would take a whole book!" In my practice, I encounter mainly people who believe in a natural and holistic lifestyle. Therefore, I'd like to discuss "natural" puppy nutrition.

In China, it's believed that to be a good doctor you also have to be a good cook. From my own experience, I know that choosing the right nourishment can support the healing of many ills. The only way we take energy into our bodies is by eating, drinking, and breathing. It's hard to change the polluted air we breath, which makes it important to take care of our nutrition.

In my experience, breed-related illnesses in dogs are on the rise, and therefore dog owners should give their puppies the healthiest and strongest possible start in life. I believe that the nutrition needs of each breed should be considered individually, as well as the dog's size, temperament, and lifestyle (is he a working dog or a companion animal?), and the needs of the owner.

Each animal and each owner is different. An extremely busy professional who owns a dog for relaxation and pleasure

Growing puppies need energy-rich foods.

should not be expected to stand in the kitchen for hours and cook for him. To do so would only add a burden to a relationship intended to bring ease and joy.

A vegetarian who is told to feed parts of other animals to her dog will wind up feeling disgusted not only by the feeding process, but by her dog as well. And should a passionate cook who glories in spending hours preparing tasty organic meals be asked to open a can of dog food? Inconceivable!

Tips for a Proper Diet

The first goal in the nutrition of a young animal is to support the development of a strong and healthy digestive system. This requires a high-quality and easily digestible diet.

The ratio of meat-to-feed depends on the temperament and growth rate of a dog's breed but should not exceed 33 percent: a good division of ingredients would be a diet that consists of one-third meat, one-third vegetables or fruit, and one-third grain.

Rice or other grains are most easily digested if they are cooked for several hours in plenty of water. Millet or brown millet is high in silica content, and therefore supportive in the development of connective tissue. These grains would be particularly good for breeds known to have difficulties with joint inflammation. Kuzu, a Japanese root sold in most health food stores, is also helpful, as it prevents

The number of treats fed during training should be subtracted from daily food rations.

diarrhea and regulates appetite.

Joint dysplasia is a common ailment in dogs. According to Chinese medicine, bone strength is governed by the universal element of "Water," so I recommend adding to your puppy's diet such "Water" category items as fish, algae, and legumes.

Growth is associated with the universal element of "Wood," which governs the strength of tendons and cartilage. A few fresh dandelion leaves finely chopped, broccoli, or green lettuce support the healthy function of this element.

Again, there is a category in the practice of Chinese medicine called "Cool Foods." Very "cooling" foods, such as citrus fruits or milk products, should be avoided as they can weaken the digestive system and deplete energy over time.

If your puppy's diet consists mainly of dry or canned food, it's important to be aware of the percentage and quality of the meat in these products, which can both be low. Read the ingredients label carefully and make sure that the product is not composed mainly of grain plus fillers made of sugar beet remnants, etc. Packaged food should contain no artificial coloring, chemical taste enhancers, or preservatives, as these can be damaging to the liver and kidneys. (Such sub-

A diet consisting of 30 percent meat is recommended for all puppies.

stances are usually identifiable by an "E" and a three-digit number.) If you're using packaged products, don't add extra vitamins and minerals because the product already contains an exactly calibrated amount and more would disturb the balance. Too high a dose of vitamin and mineral supplements are detrimental to young dogs already in a phase of rapid growth. Also, never feed a puppy sugar, margarine, or trans-fats.

Remember to view your dog as an individual being. I'm sure you have favorite meals and also enjoy a change of menu; well, just like you, your dog also has his preferences, needs, and desires. I'm confident that with sensitivity and a sensible outlook, you will put together a diet for your puppy that will suit him perfectly.

Veterinarian and TTEAM practitioner, Martina Simmerer.

The First Days at Home

A puppy's first days and nights in a strange new home can be stressful for him. In order to make the transition easier, it's a good idea to free yourself from work or obligations so that you can devote yourself to him. If that's not possible, arrange to bring him home on a weekend, or have a reliable person pay attention to him during the day until you get home. Under no circumstances should you leave your puppy alone in the house all day.

Take note of your usual daily basic activities. It's helpful to list them, for instance: getting up, meals, work, leisure time, bedtime. Then create a schedule listing the times these events occur, placing them in a column. Make a new column next to it for your puppy, so you can coordinate your life with what you would like to do with your dog and the best time to do it (see p. 68).

Since your dog will participate in

your future life, you will be teaching him to adapt to your needs; however, it's really important to be sensitive to his well-being, too. You'll find an example of what a daily routine might look like on p. 68.

If the puppy is going to be part of a family, clarify who is responsible for him. In the first days, the person who deals with and takes care of him the most should also be the one who will be most responsible for him in the future. At first, the puppy needs the chance to bond closely with that one important person. TTouch helps with this process and also with establishing a close connection with the other members of the family. I've observed many times that dogs who experience TTouch are quick to trust and connect to others who also use TTouch with them.

Be careful not to demand too much from your puppy. You may not notice when he is tired and overstimulated, because he will be delighted to be active and play as long as you are willing. I recommend that you put the puppy in his crate for periods of rest (see p. 74), which will also ensure that he doesn't injure himself by being overactive.

Very light, soft TTouches on the eyes create trust.

TTouch strengthens emotional and physical balance.

Your Daily Schedule

Below is a sample daily plan for a person who can either stay at home with a 12-week-old puppy or bring him along to a workplace. Of course, this is just an example, and you should create a schedule that fits your own life.

Time	Person	Puppy
6:00 A.M.	Wake up	Housetraining walk, playtime, 3 minutes of TTouch
7:00	Breakfast	Breakfast (first meal), housetraining walk, rest for digestion, walk to work
8:00	Begin work	3 minutes of TTouch, rest time
9:00		Rest time
10:00		Second breakfast (second meal), TTouch, playtime
11:00		Rest time
12:00 P.M.		Rest time
1:00	Lunch break	Lunch (third meal), housetraining walk, TTouch, 30 minutes rest for digestion
2:00		Rest time
3:00	Coffee break	Housetraining walk
4:00		Rest time
5:00	Leave work	Walk home
6:00		3 minutes of TTouch, playtime
7:00	Dinner	Dinner (fourth meal), housetraining walk, rest for digestion
8:00		Rest time
11:00		Housetraining walk, 2 minutes of TTouch
12:00 A.M.	Bedtime	Bedtime

The First Night

As previously mentioned, your puppy should sleep in his crate. Before you go to bed, take him out for a walk so he can relieve himself. If you take him out at midnight, he probably won't need to empty his bladder again till morning and will sleep through the rest of the night. It's a good idea for the first few nights to bring the crate into your bedroom and have the puppy sleep there. That way, you'll be instantly aware if he needs to go out. When he is older and has settled in you can move his sleeping area elsewhere, if you wish.

Even if you decide to allow your puppy to sleep in your bed, you should teach him to feel comfortable and at home in his

With TTouch, your puppy will learn to relax and go to sleep in his crate or basket.

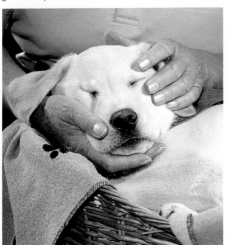

> **TTOUCH TIP**

Abalone TTouch, p. 31
Lying Leopard TTouch, p. 28
Mouth TTouch, p. 41
Ear TTouch, p. 42
Tail TTouch, p. 45

crate so that he'll be prepared for times of separation. Your puppy should learn early to feel safe without you and to trust the people who are looking after him.

Feeding Time

Choose a quiet spot in your home for your dog to eat his meals, one where he will not be disturbed. Hold the food bowl in your hands and ask him to "Sit," and "Stay" (see p. 98). Actually, your puppy will enjoy this, and you'll be surprised how quickly he'll learn. Teach him through your voice, eye contact, and body language. Say the words "Sit," and "Stay," in a friendly tone instead of one that sounds like a military command. Begin with training your puppy to sit. When he does what you've asked, praise him effusively. Express your delight with compliments like, "Thank you!" "That was great!" or "What a good dog!"

You can then ask him to "Wait," or "Stay," accompanied by a hand signal.

"Stay," with hand signals.

After he has sat quietly for a moment, put his bowl down on the floor and release him with an appropriate hand signal, tone of voice, or body language and a word like "Okay."

When you establish this routine as a regular mealtime ritual, your puppy will regard it as play and look forward to it with special pleasure. Simultaneously, he'll be learning basic rules of behavior. His water dish, however, should be kept filled and freely accessible to him at all times. Your dog should not be disturbed while he is eating or drinking.

Housetraining

Litters born and raised in a household are generally housebroken by their mother, who demonstrates the proper behavior by example. After a time, the little ones learn the lesson.

If your puppy has been raised in a breeder's home rather than in a kennel, there's a very good chance that he will not "go" in the house. However, if the puppy was separated from his mother too early, he will not yet have learned to be "clean." Normally though, by the time your puppy comes to live with you, he'll know that he must not urinate or defecate in the house.

Nevertheless, have a good carpet cleaner ready, because your new arrival will have "accidents." This can be due to excitement, insecurity, separation from his mother and siblings, unfamiliar surroundings, and having to "hold it" for longer than he can. After all, he is a still an untrained young animal, so it's up to you to take care and to notice when he is giving you signals that he needs to go out. He may stare at you, get restless, or start looking for places to go. He'll also need to go out after a period of hard play. If he has an accident, don't punish him—doing so will only create tension in your dog. Remember, if your dog makes a mistake, roll up a newspaper and whack yourself,

>**TTOUCH TIP**

Ear TTouch, p. 42
Belly Lift, p. 44

When beginning to take housetraining walks, it's safe and helpful to use a dog harness and double leash to teach the puppy how to walk on a lead. Puppies are easily distracted and this method immediately corrects them when they begin to pull. The Wand (p. 95) supports one-handed leading. Here, a young Australian Sheepdog learns how to walk in a balanced way while on the lead.

because you just were not paying enough attention.

Puppies are still babies and need a chance to relieve themselves many times a day and perhaps at night. In the beginning of training, you might have to get up at night, should the dog signal that he needs to go out. Usually, a final midnight trip outside will suffice until 6:00 A.M., when he'll need to be walked once again. Ask the breeder if he takes his puppies out at night.

Housetraining Walks

It's a good idea to take your puppy out on a leash immediately after every meal, so that he doesn't make a "mistake" in the house. Walk with an easy, steady pace and praise the puppy generously after he has "done his business." If it turns out that he doesn't need to relieve himself, bring him back home, put him into his crate, and after a while, go out with him once more.

Gentle Belly Lifts (p. 44) enhance digestion.

The Lying Leopard TTouch (p. 28) on the belly.

Keep your dog on a short leash so that he can't run or play, thus keeping him concentrated on his task. Show your dog the right place to "do his business." Some dogs don't like to be observed relieving themselves and prefer going under a bush or disappearing behind a fence. Respect your puppy's preference and take him to a suitable spot. Encourage him to urinate or defecate and then stand by patiently until he is done.

Belly Lifts (p. 44) and *Ear TTouches* (p. 42) help to stimulate elimination. Establishing code words—for instance, "Pee-time," or "Go-poop,"—can also be useful. Remember to be patient with your puppy and to praise him heartily when he has done his "job."

> **>TTOUCH TIP**
>
> *Balance Leash, p. 105*
> *Ground Surfaces, p. 119*

Walking on a Leash

The first walks with your little dog should be short: acquaint him with your street or take him once around the block. This should suffice for the first few days of outside adventures. In my experience, it is better for most puppies and dogs to be led using a dog harness rather than a collar and leash.

I also believe that one should allow a dog to sniff around as much as he likes. This is especially true for young dogs, as it is their way of learning to trust and familiarize themselves with their new environment. Through sniffing the urine traces of other dogs, they are receiving messages that tell them "this is a good place." Allowing the dog to do this is not a failing on your part: instead, you are actually being aware and considerate of the natural needs of your animal. When you wish to move on, get your puppy's attention by using your voice or giving him a treat or toy. As soon as he turns back to you, give him plenty of praise. Every experience with you should be a positive one, then, in the future he will be motivated to pay attention to your voice and requests. Praise him, even for just walking on.

From the first walk, avoid situations in which your dog can pull on the leash. When you pull an animal on a lead, they will always react by pulling back. As soon as you pull on him, your dog will pull against you even more. Therefore, your dog should associate your subtle signals on the leash as a message to immediately stop pulling and to release pressure on the lead. When signaling, let your hands and arms feel soft and loose and breathe evenly and without tension.

Meeting Other Dogs

Many puppy owners find an encounter with other dogs stressful, because it's always uncertain how the dogs will react to each other.

Dogs want to get together, to greet and sniff each other. However, what you want is to be in control of the situation. What to do?

When meeting stranger dogs, your little puppy will not be privy to the so-called "puppy protection" that occurs as

This young terrier has a tendency to pull on the lead; he is not in balance.

> **>TTOUCH TIP**

Playground for Higher Learning, p. 113

Pausing for a mutual snuggle strengthens your bond.

a natural phenomenon within a canine family or an adult pack whose members are known to each other. Therefore, it's important that you know how to protect your puppy in case the need arises. On the other hand, your dog must be able to have fun and to connect with other dogs.

The best thing is to keep your puppy on the leash and your eye on the situation. When large dogs approach, keep your puppy's safety in mind. Encountering this bigger creature, the puppy may feel threatened and therefore take a defensive posture, leaving himself no avenue of escape. Pay attention to the strange dog's behavior, because he may not realize that your dog is a baby, and he may react aggressively or with play that is too rough. Even a swipe with a paw that is meant to be harmless and friendly can injure a puppy.

If your dog is a small breed, don't hesitate to assure his safety by lifting him up into your arms. Stay in control of the situation without becoming stressed, so that your puppy will not learn to be nervous around large or unfamiliar dogs.

Rest Breaks

To aid digestion, to rest, and to sleep, put your puppy into his open crate. Dogs doze, rest, or sleep up to 17 hours a day! To prevent unnecessary stress, make sure your puppy or adult dog receives this (astonishing) amount of downtime.

If your puppy wants contact with you during or after rest periods, do TTouches on him while you hold him in your lap or lie next to him on the floor. During the puppy's first days, it's good to be as close and cozy as possible with him. This will not only help to create a deep bond between you, but is natural for the pup; it's what he would be experiencing were he still with his mother and siblings.

Visiting Friends

When taking your dog along to visit friends, bring his trusty blanket with you—it will make him feel secure enough to lie down and rest. Pick a place for him near you and keep him safely on the leash. If he's restless (and it's not because he needs to pee), calm him down with TTouch. Ask your friends (should they seem interested) if they'd like to try TTouch on him too. It's a good way for the

Praise your dog with TTouch.

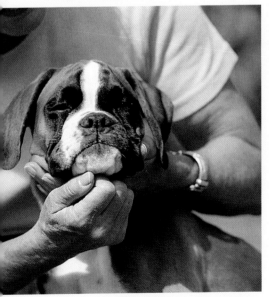

puppy to become accustomed to contact with other people and is helpful as preparation for a visit to the vet.

If your friends have children, show them how to do the TTouch, and then let each of them try it on your puppy—under your supervision, of course. Offering treats to the puppy is a great way for kids and dog to make friends; however, your dog may feel insecure with children. If this is the case, get the kids to put the treats on the floor first, before approaching the dog. Demonstrate how to offer the treat to the dog in the flattened palm of the hand.

Puppy Play Groups

There's a lot to be said for enrolling your puppy in the puppy play group at a dog school. Young dogs need contact with others of the same age: through play, they educate each other in canine socialization. You too, will feel stimulated and discover new ways to play with your puppy since the group program also includes play between the owners and their dogs.

Visit the dog schools in your area and make sure the dogs are separated according to size. Sometimes, when a smaller puppy is engaged in off-leash play with larger young dogs, the larger ones will dominate the smaller "underdog" and ignore the little one's surrender signals. This can lead to frustration and aggres-

Training with a "puppy play group" is fun and enhances a dog's social skills.

sion on the part of the smaller dog. See to it that when playing off-leash your puppy is not always on the defensive.

There is probably a TTEAM-oriented dog school or a TTEAM practitioner in your neighborhood who can recommend the right situation for you and your puppy.

> **>TTOUCH TIP**

Lying Leopard TTouch, p. 28
Ear TTouch, p. 42
Mouth TTouch, p. 41
Tarantulas Pulling the Plow, p. 38
Abalone TTouch, p. 31
Raccoon TTouch, p. 30

Off-Leash Play in a Puppy Group
by **Sarah Marsh**
Dog Trainer and TTEAM Practitioner, Great Britain

Dogs mainly communicate with each other through body language and subtle signals. These signals, central in avoiding conflict, often go unnoticed by owners, but they are an important part of a puppy's education in canine socialization and hierarchy.

Puppy play groups can be an ideal and safe environment for puppies to test their social competence. However, groups that are not separated by size and developmental stage present a definite risk. Groups should be comprised of

no more than five dogs under the age of 18 months. It's essential to observe the puppies' behavior as they play, making sure that they are not intimidated, overwhelmed, or tyrannizing other dogs.

Another good group activity is for puppies to learn to be led by their owners. Wearing a dog harness and a leash, the puppy is taught to walk with his owner in a self-controlled and well-balanced way. Using only a collar and leash is not advisable.

A puppy with a strong body and high energy needs this type of leading in order to play safely with dogs who are smaller or weaker. If play becomes too high-spirited, ask your dog to lie down. Then, calm him by changing the angle of his tail or by doing the stroking *Noah's March* (p. 37) on his body.

The play periods should be short, with pauses between them in which the owner holds the puppy for a moment or two before returning him to the pack for more fun. Play should also be interrupted by the owner if one dog is pinning another down on his back for too long. The underdog must have a chance to escape; therefore, the owner of the stronger dog should remove him.

Here, the dogs at play are equally matched. They are about the same size and take turns being dominant.

>**TTOUCH TIP**

Clouded Leopard TTouch, p. 26
Lying Leopard TTouch, p. 28
Ear TTouch, p. 42
Mouth TTouch, p. 41

It's important for a puppy to play with others once a week. By the age of five months, your puppy should have a strong educational foundation.

Raising Puppies: An Overview

> The main goal of the first days spent with your dog is to establish a bond. The puppy needs and will seek a close relationship with you. Mutual trust, a basic requirement of being close, will deepen between you as you offer the puppy love and dependability. The bond between dogs and humans is a heart-to-heart relationship. However, this should not mean that your dog cannot bear to be separated from you. That's where TTouch is so helpful: it deepens the connection between you, while at the same time supporting the sense of self-reliance your dog needs for the times you can't be with him. To build closeness, do a few moments of TTouch on your puppy many times during the day.

> Demonstrating an attitude of respect toward animals is a basic principle of my work. Essential for this is being able to read and understand their lan-

The dog on the left demonstrates his dominance through his lifted tail and open mouth.

guage. Notice the ways in which your young dog uses body language to express himself.

> Keep learning sessions short and be clear and consistent so that the dog doesn't tire. Training with you should be fun for him. Remember to show him appreciation and tell him he is wonderful. It's not the treat rewards that create a deep bond between you, it's your acknowledgement and giving him TTouch that will do so.

> For me, the old saying, "A dog is a man's best friend," is no meaningless phrase—it's actually a reality! When you acknowledge your dog as a friend, you become a team.

> Make clear to your dog what you want from him in a friendly and patient manner. Many misunderstandings in training happen because people don't understand that a young animal needs time to process what is being asked of him. Too many demands given too quickly will confuse him. Patience and simple, clear communication are important ingredients for success in raising your puppy.

A puppy can learn even by watching.

Caring for Your Puppy

Caring for Your Puppy's Coat

The coat of a long-haired dog needs regular care to keep it from matting. It's especially important to brush a long-haired dog when he is shedding; getting rid of the old fur permits a new coat to grow without problems. Keep bathing to a minimum so that the fur retains its texture and ability to keep the dog warm and his skin protected against dirt.

When bathing, use a shampoo that supports the health of his fur and skin. Mixing shampoo with water before you massage it into the fur prevents dogs with sensitive skin from being irritated.

Use TTouch before brushing and trimming as a pleasant way to promote your puppy's self-confidence and prepare him for his "health and beauty" session. *Hair Slides* (p. 39) are a good way to accustom a dog to fur care. Doing *Hair Slides* prior to trimming a long-haired dog also gives you the opportunity to pull out the loose wooly sections of the undercoat.

Brushing time can be an enjoyable experience for you and your dog. When brushing a puppy, don't be in a hurry—take your time so as not to alarm him. This is a wonderful opportunity to deepen your relationship with him.

Some dogs are more sensitive than others. When people come to me with dogs that refuse to be brushed, I often find that the problem is simple—the animals are being brushed too roughly and too fast. If, when you brush your dog, he

If your puppy reacts sensitively when brushed, stroke carefully using only the back of the brush. TTouches impart a feeling of security.

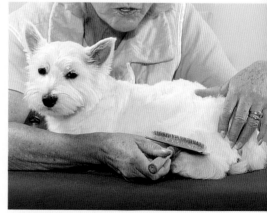

>TTOUCH TIP

Clouded Leopard TTouch, p. 26

Hair Slides, p. 39

Python TTouch, p. 34

Coiled Python TTouch, p. 32

Raccoon TTouch, p. 30

Tarantulas Pulling the Plow, p. 38

Paw TTouch, p. 46

twitches his skin, won't stand still, or tries to run off, it's probably because you are not aware that he's very sensitive. Do *Tarantulas Pulling the Plow* (p. 38), lift the skin lightly with the hair, make slow *circular* TTouches (p. 26), and end with *Hair Slides*.

TTouch and slow brushing is a good way to prepare your puppy for a visit to

Slow and careful brushing can be a pleasant experience for a young pup.

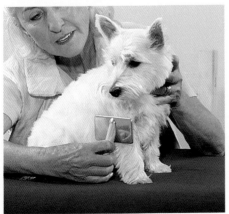

the groomer.

In rainy weather, you'll be glad when your puppy calmly allows you to dry his legs, paws and entire body before he goes into the house. To get him used to this routine, I would suggest working his legs with the *Python TTouch* (p. 34) and his feet with the *Paw TTouch* (p. 46).

Visiting a Groomer

Regular hair care and TTouch sessions prepare your puppy for being handled by the groomer as well as by other unfamiliar people. TTouch increases your puppy's self-confidence. However, on his first visit to the groomer, it's best to stay with him until you see that he feels secure in his new environment. Choose a groomer who is concerned and mindful when working with dogs. If the groomer shows interest, demonstrate different TTouches for him or her. I know a number of groomers who have added TTouch to their practice because they discovered it makes their work easier.

Tooth Care

Every puppy needs to grow accustomed to having his teeth brushed as well as examined. When evaluating show dogs for prizes, the judges generally include an inspection of a candidate's mouth and teeth. Schedule your dog for an annual visit to a veterinarian for a dental check.

Lying Leopard TTouches (p. 28) on the mouth, Raccoon TTouches (p. 30) on the gums, and finally introducing the toothbrush by contacting the puppy's body.

Some breeds get more tartar build-up than others and should therefore visit the veterinarian more frequently. Brushing the dog's teeth, giving him rope chews, and maintaining him on a healthy diet can aid in keeping teeth healthy and tartar free.

The mouth is connected to the limbic system in the brain, the site which regulates emotion. Gentle *Mouth TTouches* (p. 41) can therefore act as a positive influence on your puppy's emotional outlook. *Lying Leopard* (p. 28) and *Mouth TTouches* prepare a dog to accept contact on and in the mouth without stress.

When your puppy is in the teething phase, offer him rope chews or bones to bite and gnaw. *Raccoon TTouches* (p. 30) on the puppy's gums help to keep him from chewing your furniture or other forbidden objects. *Mouth TTouches* with a

> ### >TTOUCH TIP
>
> *Lying Leopard TTouch, p. 28*
> *Mouth TTouch, p. 41*
> *Raccoon TTouch, p. 30*

soft, cool wash rag also help ease teething problems.

Nail Clipping

It's easy to forget to clip your dog's nails, but it's an important health measure that when regularly attended to, can actually lengthen your animal's life. When the nails grow too long, they curve back under the paws, not allowing your dog to walk normally. The dog shifts his weight to the back of the paw, resulting in tension and imbalance. With TTouch, your puppy learns to relax his legs and paws

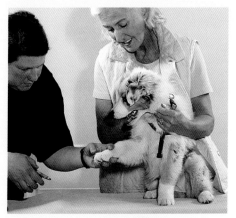

for treatment, something which does not come naturally him.

If you can hear your dog's nails clicking on a smooth surface, it's time to check their length. When your dog is standing still, his nails should not reach the ground. Unless you are experienced, leave the nail clipping job to the veterinarian or groomer. If you are inexperienced and attempt to do it yourself, you might clip the nails too short.

›TTOUCH TIP

Coiled Python TTouch, p. 32
Python TTouch, p. 34
Raccoon TTouch, p. 30
Paw TTouch, p. 46

TTouch on the front and back legs prepares the puppy for nail clipping. Do not clip the nails yourself unless you are very experienced.

Tick Control

When the weather is warm, checking for tick bites becomes a matter of everyday life. A single bite can infect both humans and dogs with Lyme disease, a dangerous bacterial infection. If your dog becomes ill after being bitten by a tick, take him to the vet to be tested.

In spring and summer, check your dog daily for ticks and remove them immediately. Special, easy-to-use tweezers are available at pet supply stores. Unfortunately, insect-repellent collars, sprays, and shampoos do not offer 100-percent protection against ticks, and some of these products can actually be harmful to both humans and dogs.

Accustom your dog to the daily rite of "tick search and removal." Of course, this procedure will be much easier for you if your dog is lying down or standing quietly. Through TTouch sessions, the dog will learn to relax during the process.

Taking Your Puppy's Temperature

Use a rectal thermometer to get a precise reading of your puppy's body temperature.

Even before the puppy's first visit to the vet, work with him so that he will learn to trust the procedure. Get him used to having you touch his hindquarters and to standing still for several minutes.

In order to make the rectal insertion easier, smear a little petroleum jelly on the tip of the thermometer. Modern digital thermometers are thin, unbreakable, precise, and easy-to-read. Normal body temperature for a dog is between 99 and 102.5 degrees F.

> **>TTOUCH TIP**
>
> *Noah's March, p. 37*
> *Raccoon TTouch, p. 30*
> *Tarantulas Pulling the Plow, p. 38*

Gentle preparation for tick removal.

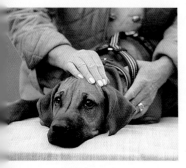

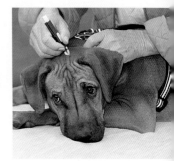

Taking your puppy's temperature is easier if you prepare him with TTouches on his hindquarters.

The *Tail TTouch* (p. 45) as well as the *Python* and *Raccoon Touches* (pp. 34 and 30) around the anus are especially effective in preparing you dog to accept the thermometer.

> **TTOUCH TIP**

Raccoon TTouch, p. 30
Python TTouch, p. 34
Tail TTouch, p. 45

Visiting the Veterinarian

Many veterinarians around the world have become familiar with TTEAM and TTouch and use the Tellington Method with great success to support and complement their medical practice. In her article *Tellington TTEAM in Veterinary Practice*, Daniela Zurr, DVM, describes the many possible ways that a veterinarian can apply the system to his or her work.

As your puppy's owner, there's a great deal you can do to keep him healthy. Visits to the vet are an integral part of life with your dog, and preparing him for the experience is yet another way of caring for him.

> Stroking the ears as in the *Ear TTouch* (p. 42) can be a vital tool in emergencies, such as shock or unconsciousness: I've actually saved the lives of both humans and animals by applying the *Ear TTouch* until medical help could arrive, or while on the way to the hospital. Over time, I've received many reports from others who have had similar experiences using TTouch.

> The *Ear TTouch* is usually helpful in

preparing your puppy for a veterinary examination, and especially for ear inspections. It also relieves pain and intestinal or stomach aches or cramps. The *Ear TTouch* serves to stabilize breathing and circulation.

> *Ear TTouches* and *Coiled Python TTouches* (p. 32) relax your puppy on the trip to the vet's office, in the waiting room, and during examinations and medical treatments. In addition, it's an opportunity for you to aid your dog instead of standing helplessly by.

> The *Body Wrap* (p. 87) or *T-Shirt* (p. 88) helps an anxious or hyperactive puppy feel consciously secure within his own body while he's on the way to the vet or in the waiting room.

>TTOUCH TIP

Ear TTouch, p. 42
Lying Leopard TTouch, p. 28
Coiled Python TTouch, p. 32
Body Wrap, p. 87
T-Shirt, p. 88

The Ear TTouch (p. 42) is an important first-aid emergency measure.

Leaving Your Puppy Home Alone

At first, it's best not to leave your puppy at home alone. However, after you have established a solid bond, you'll need to prepare your dog for the inevitable times when he must be on his own.

Begin by leaving him alone for short periods after he's walked or played, and when it's natural for him to take a rest. Put time-consuming and interesting toys (such as a Kong® full of treats) in his crate. Calm, soft music playing while you're away will have a relaxing affect on the puppy.

I think it's important and helpful to tell the puppy that you're leaving and to give him a task—for example, tell him, "Take good care of your toys." Say goodbye quietly and in a soft voice. The more quietly positive you are and the calmer the images in your mind, the calmer and quieter your dog will remain while you're gone. When you return, greet him softly, sending out the message that it's absolutely normal for him to have behaved well while he was alone.

Prepare him in advance by putting him in his closed crate a number of times a day when you are present in the room with him. Next, lengthen the time he's in his crate, then leave the room, and eventually, the house. If you don't make a fuss, your puppy will learn to feel happy and secure in his own little den. Puppies often become overstimulated when left alone with access to the whole house. This makes them feel insecure, and the resultant stress acts on the bladder and digestive tract.

If you have a puppy that continues to be nervous about being alone, patiently begin the training over again.

Body Wrap

Body Wraps intensify your puppy's sense of his own body, enabling him to feel more certain of his movements and behavior. Young dogs who fear loud noises

> TTOUCH TIP

Circular TTouches, p. 26
Ear TTouch, p. 42
Mouth TTouch, p. 41
Tail TTouch, p. 45
Body Wrap, p. 87
Belly Lift, p. 44
T-Shirt, p. 88

> TTOUCH TIP

Tarantulas Pulling the Plow, p. 38
Lick of the Cow's Tongue, p. 36

How to apply the Body Wrap, step-by-step.

or who are nervous in a car, improve when wearing the *Body Wrap*.

For the *Body Wrap*, you can use elastic bandages bought at a pharmacy (see photos). Place the middle of the bandage across the dog's chest and then bring the ends up to cross over on the back. Now, take the ends again, bring them down to wrap once under the torso, and then bring them up over the back. Tie them there with a knot, or secure them with a safety pin. Make sure that the bandage lies flat and is neither too loose nor too tight.

T-Shirt

T-Shirts enhance a dog's sense of his own body, creating a positive self-awareness that is especially helpful in overcoming fear and nervousness. You'll find that most pet stores carry a great variety of easy-on and easy-off dog shirts in many sizes. The step-by-step photo series illustrates how to put a *T-Shirt* on your dog.

> **›TTOUCH TIP**
>
> *Tarantulas Pulling the Plow, p. 38*
> *Lick of the Cow's Tongue, p. 36*

Put the T-Shirt on your dog slowly and carefully, so that he learns to like wearing it. First, put both front legs through the arm holes, then pull the neck opening over the head, and finally pull the T-Shirt down over the body.

The *T-Shirt* is helpful when your puppy is overexcited, lacks self-confidence or is timid, or for training in the Playground for Higher Learning (p. 113). How long to leave the shirt on depends on the situation. The puppy should wear it only under supervision.

Caring for a Bitch and Her Puppies

If you are breeding dogs, you'll find TTouch can do a great deal to ease a mother's pregnancy and labor. I've had the privilege of being present at many births, and each time, I was newly awed

>TTOUCH TIP

Belly Lift, p. 44
Lying Leopard TTouch, p. 28
Coiled Python TTouch, p. 32
Ear TTouch, p. 42
Mouth TTouch, p. 41
Raccoon TTouch, p. 30

A proud Afghan mother with her litter.

by the power of nature. With TTouch, you can not only be present for this miracle, but you can give gentle support and ease the pain of labor.

Many people have begun using TTouch on the pregnant mother's belly to make contact with puppies in *utero*. I've received

>LINDA'S TIP

If a female dog reacts nervously to being bred, Ear TTouch, Tail TTouch, Python TTouch on the thighs, Paw TTouch and Tarantulas Pulling the Plow are all useful ways to strengthen her self-confidence.

wonderful reports of young animals who were TTouched while in the womb and were then born with an unusual ability to trust and bond with humans.

During a bitch's pregnancy, you can use gentle *Belly Lifts* (p. 44) to help relieve the pressure on her abdomen. *Lying Leopard TTouches* (p. 28) and *Coiled Python TTouches* (p. 32) on the nipple area prepare the mother for nursing her litter.

Ear TTouches (p. 42) are beneficial during pregnancy and labor, helping respiration and circulation.

Should a mother not accept her pups, slow and connected *Lying Leopard TTouches* over the whole body as well *Ear* and *Mouth TTouches*, are helpful in restoring her emotional balance. The limbic system in the brain regulates emotional response and is connected to the mouth, therefore gentle *Mouth TTouches* can have a positive effect on the mother's emotional state.

Making *Lying Leopard TTouches* on the teats with a warm washcloth soothes sore nipples and stretched skin. If a puppy refuses to nurse or doesn't suck strongly enough, TTouches on his mouth, gums, and tongue will activate and strengthen the sucking reflex. *Ear TTouches* and *Raccoon TTouches* (p. 30) over the entire body "awaken" the puppy and support his circulatory system.

Ear TTouch (p. 42).

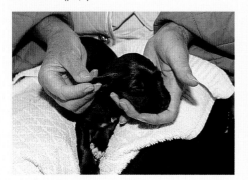

Mouth TTouch (p. 41).

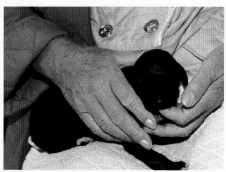

Belly Lift (p. 44).

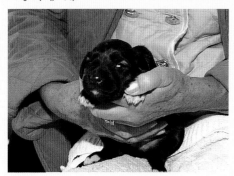

Tail TTouch (p. 45).

TTouch Training and Learning Exercises

Equipment for the Playground for Higher Learning

Collar: I recommend using a wide, smooth, flat collar—never a choke collar.

The Halti head collar or canine halter.

Halti/Snoot Loop Head Collar or Canine Halter: There is a wide variety of head collars for dogs (canine halters) that can be very useful for mature dogs. They include the Halti, Snoot Loop, and Gentle Leader®, to name a few. These head collars, when combined with a harness (or in some cases, a flat collar) and a double-ended leash (one with a snap at each end—see this page), allow you to gently guide and influence your dog using both hands. They come in various sizes and styles, and should fit comfortably without sliding around on the head. I rarely use a head collar for puppies, but on larger, rambunctious and older puppies, a head collar combined with a harness or flat collar, and a double-ended leash can be effective (see p. 108).

Leash: Use a leash that is 6 feet long, flat, and has snaps on both ends. One end can then be attached to the harness and the other to the collar, so that the dog can be led in balance when you use both hands—one hand influencing the harness and the other signaling on the collar. I use the two-handed approach to leash training, as it permits you to signal the dog with greater sensitivity, subtlety, and effectiveness than with one lead only.

Dog Harness: It's usually safer to attach a puppy's lead to a harness than to a collar: the pull of the lead on the collar can harm a dog's spinal column, particularly the fragile neck vertebrae where pressure from the leash is most concentrated. The combination of harness and flat collar teaches dogs to listen to more subtle signals on the leash.

There are many different styles of harness now available. I favor a "step-in"

The "step-in" dog harness.

The Body Wrap (p. 87).

harness, as shown in many of the photos (see p. 94), because the rings on the sides of the harness near the dog's shoulders give numerous options to which to attach a double-ended leash. This type of harness has a strap that runs over the back with two rings for attaching a leash. Two more rings are fastened to straps at each shoulder, and another at the chest. For this harness I recommend a leash with a snap at each end.

Wand: I use a specialized white "stick" or *wand* as an aid when training dogs to lead. I use it to stroke the body, and also to serve as a "pointer." For instance, I use a wand to help guide a puppy through such learning exercises as the *Labyrinth* or the *Board* (pp. 113 and 114).

Body Wrap: The *Body Wrap* (p. 87) enhances a dog's sense of his own body and increases his confidence in his movements and behavior. It's especially beneficial for dogs who are afraid of loud noises or who are nervous when riding in a car. The *Body Wrap* also helps injured dogs to recover. Use the elastic bandages you can find in most pharmacies (see p. 88).

T-Shirt: The *T-Shirt* for dogs is not meant as a fashion statement, but rather as an aid for puppies who are insecure and nervous (see p. 88). The shirt's tight enclosure of the body reassures the puppy and gives him a sense of safety. They come in various sizes and are available at pet supply stores.

The white wand.

The dog T-Shirt.

Sit, Down, Stay, Come, and Lead

These five exercises are important basic concepts for all dogs to understand. Your body language, a playful attitude, and plenty of praise will help your puppy learn them. For your teaching to be successful, you'll also need to be consistent and time the lessons so as not to stress the dog. Using imaging will help you create a focus for the exercises: clearly picture the progression of the exercises you wish your puppy learn.

To make descriptions of the training easier to follow, I break each exercise down into steps. For example, in the section called "Feeding Time" (see p. 69), I described how I taught a puppy to sit and wait until I put his food dish down on the floor.

I think it's best for you to do the first exercises with your puppy in your house, apartment, yard, or another enclosed area where he will not be distracted by other dogs. When teaching the puppy to sit and to lie down, it's helpful to have him practice on a piece of carpet or cloth, so that he forms a relationship with ground and "place." I first saw Australian TTEAM practitioner Andy Robertson use this technique, a method that has proven to be highly successful.

A happy puppy learns to stay in place.

Voice and hand signal: "Stay on your mat."

"On Your Mat"

It's easy and great fun to teach your dog to go to his "place"—his mat. The mat can also be used as a training aid to accustom the dog to his crate (see p. 57).

The following list of instructions was formulated by the Australian TTEAM practitioner, Andy Robertson.

> Find a piece of carpet or cloth to serve as the "mat," plus your puppy's favorite treats.

> Place the mat on the floor with your puppy on a leash. Put a treat on the mat and say, "On your mat!" while simultaneously signaling toward the mat with your arm and hand.

> Encourage your puppy to go onto the mat and eat the treats. Reward him by placing further treats on the mat.

> Call the puppy off the mat, and repeat this same exercise three to five times.

> Once the puppy has understood that he should go to the mat, while he's there, show him "Sit," and "Stay," (see p. 98). Don't forget that the exercise should only take a few seconds, after which you release your dog with words like, "Free," or "Go."

> When you ask your dog to go to the mat, he should sit at first for five seconds, then 10, and so on. Some puppies can sit longer than a few seconds at the beginning; however, make sure not to lose your dog's attention. If you advance too quickly, your puppy may not be able to retain what he's learned.

> As the training proceeds, keep reducing the arm and hand signaling, so that later just your voice cue and a small gesture with your hand will be enough.

> "On your mat" can also be used in the training for "Down," and "Stay." Once your puppy has understood that "On your mat," earns him a reward, you can add the training signals for "Down," "Stay," and "Free" (see p. 100). Keep extending the time between "Down," and "Free."

Crate and Mat

The mat can be helpful if your puppy is familiar with the "On your mat" exercise, yet reluctant to enter his crate.

> Put the mat into the crate and place a treat on it where the puppy can see it. Close the door to the crate.

> As soon as the puppy shows interest in the treat, open the door and let him go inside and get it. Leave the door open.

> After the puppy has done this several times, when he is inside, close the door for just a few seconds and then open it again.

> Gradually extend the time you keep the door closed.

Remember, the idea is to make the experience of being in the crate a pleasant one.

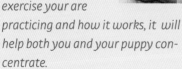

>LINDA'S TIP

If you keep a clear mental image of the exercise your are practicing and how it works, it will help both you and your puppy concentrate.

"Sit" and "Stay"

Here's an easy, friendly way to teach your puppy to sit and stay—one that he will actually enjoy.

> You'll need a dog harness, a leash, and plenty of your puppy's favorite treats, chopped small if necessary.

> Speak to your puppy in a friendly way and say his name. Gain his full attention.

> Take a piece of treat the size of a pea and hold it close to your puppy's nose. While he's concentrating on the treat, pass your hand over his head back between his ears. His nose will follow your hand, which will push his head back, shifting his balance so that he has to sit down.

> The minute he sits, give the puppy the treat. Say the word "Sit," only when the puppy has sat and not before: that way he'll make the connection between the word and the action.

> Repeat the exercise five times.

Should your puppy try to move backward, do the exercise in a corner where he doesn't have that option. If the puppy jumps up, then you're probably holding the treat too high. Hold it close to and right above his nose.

> Once the treat-and-sit routine is well established, you can introduce the voice cue. Say the word "Sit," and once again, hold the treat close to the puppy's nose and pass it over his head

so that he sits. Don't repeat the voice cue—if you catch yourself doing it, mentally count to 10 before you begin the exercise again. This gives the puppy a chance to react to your cue.

> After the puppy has learned to "Sit," at your voice cue, he's ready to learn "Stay." As soon as the dog sits, say "Wait," or "Stay," and reward him so that he remains sitting. Repeat the voice cue three to five times while feeding him a treat each time. Then release him from the lesson with "Free," or "Go."

> Every time you do the sitting exercise with your puppy, say "Stay," and give him a reward. Very gradually, lengthen the pause between the word "Stay," and the treat reward.

Your puppy might run off before, or as soon as he has received his reward—both reactions are fine. Just keep on practicing the exercise and praising him.

You can now include the "Sit," and "Stay," exercises in your daily routine.

The treat is held close to the puppy's nose and passed back over his head.

As soon as the puppy sits, immediately praise him and give him the treat.

"Down" and "Stay"

When your dog has mastered "Sit," and "Stay," and you've established the signals, you can begin training him "Down," and "Stay." These requests are useful when you want to prevent your puppy from running off, or you'd like him to lie still for a while.

> You'll need the dog harness, leash, treats, and possibly the mat as well (see p. 97).

> With the puppy in a standing position, hold a piece of treat about the size of a pea a fraction of an inch from his nose. When he has focused on the treat, bring your hand down to the ground. The puppy will follow the treat down with his nose and body, and in most cases, will end up lying down.

> You can also begin with your dog in a sitting position, and bring his nose down with the same hand gesture.

> Using a soft or smooth surface when practicing this exercise will make it easier for the puppy to learn.

> As soon as the puppy lies down, praise him and give him the treat. Repeat the exercise five times.

> When you are consistently getting the puppy into the "Down," position, it is time to add the cue word, "Down." Say "Down," take the treat down to the ground and he will go into the down position. Take care not to repeat the

Step-by-step, the puppy goes from sitting to lying down.

>LINDA'S TIP

When a puppy is concentrating too hard on a treat, he forgets to think. TTouch teaches him to behave with conscious awareness rather than with instinctive conditioning. Through TTouch, your puppy will grow to be an intelligent and delightful companion.

word over and over. Count to 10 silently between each of the times you say the cue. This will give the puppy time to respond.

> Once the puppy has consistently responded to "Down," you can introduce the word "Stay." Immediately after you've said "Stay," and while your dog is still lying down, reward him with the treat. Repeat this exercise three to five times. Then release the puppy with the word "Free." Practice this exercise daily to impress it upon the dog.
> After the puppy has mastered the ex-

>TTOUCH TIP

Lying Leopard TTouch, p. 28
Tarantulas Pulling the Plow, p. 38
Ear TTouch, p. 42

ercise, you can begin to substitute three or four *circular* TTouches (p. 26) and words of praise in place of the treats. The *circular* TTouches deepen the bond with your dog, while at the same time he learns not to fixate on the treat as a reward.

"Come"

> The equipment needed is the same as in the previous exercises.
> Ask a friend or an assistant to stand about 10 feet away from the puppy. The distance depends on the size of the puppy; for a little Fox Terrier it would probably be about 7½ feet; for a Dalmatian, 10½ feet. Have your puppy on a leash snapped to a dog harness.
> Your assistant will call the puppy by name to attract his attention, and the dog will then want to run to the person. Free the dog from the leash so that he can run to the assistant. As the puppy runs to him, the assistant continues to call his name, interspersed with interesting sounds, for instance clicking with the tongue, whistling, or tapping on the ground.
> When the puppy arrives at the assistant's feet, the assistant takes the leash and rewards the dog with a treat.
> Repeat the exercise, but this time re-

verse it so that it is you who are calling the dog to come to you.

> Repeat the entire exercise three to five times. If you do this exercise daily, the dog will run to the person calling him faster and faster. If you don't like using treats, you can reward the dog with a few circular TTouches under the chin and/or with words of praise like "Good boy."

> Once the puppy has perfected this exercise and comes to you and your assistant when called, you can add "Sit," and "Down." Finish the session by releasing the puppy with the words, "Free," or "Go."

"Stay," using voice and hand cues.

"Stay"

"Stay" is an excellent way for your puppy to learn that he can be near you without following you around.

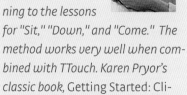

>LINDA'S TIP

You might want to add Clicker Training to the lessons for "Sit," "Down," and "Come." The method works very well when combined with TTouch. Karen Pryor's classic book, Getting Started: Clicker Training for Dogs, *would be a good choice to give you some basics.*

> This exercise can be taught with or without a leash. Have plenty of your puppy's favorite treats on hand.

> Use the words "Wait," or "Stay," as the cue and reinforce this with a hand signal: hold you hand up with the palm facing the puppy so that he can see it.

> You can teach the puppy this exercise while he's on his mat, when he's sitting or lying down on his bed, or anywhere that you find convenient.

> Ask your puppy to "Sit," and when he does, give him a treat. Show the puppy the hand signal, and in a normal voice, say "Wait," or "Stay." Reward him with a treat.

> Practice this routine several times daily. Gradually allow more and more time to elapse between the voice cue and the treat. End each session with the release word, "Free."

> In later sessions, keep lengthening the time between your voice cue and the reward treat.

"Stay" with Distance

> While your puppy remains sitting in place, take a small step backward and repeat the cue, "Stay," or "Wait." Then say "Stay," or "Wait," step forward to your original position, tell him he's a "Good dog," and give him a treat. Release the puppy saying, "Free."

> As soon as your puppy is familiar with your forward and backward movements and sits quietly for them, you can start stepping from side to side.

> Remember the sequence: say the puppy's name, followed by "Sit"; pause; say "Good dog"; then, "Stay"; and reward with a treat. Then, step sideways to the right or left. Stop. Say your puppy's name followed by the cue, "Stay." Then go back to your original place in front of the puppy, while saying, "Stay," his name and "Good dog." Now it's time to give him his treat, and end by saying, "Free."

> If this exercise is successful, begin the next stage: make a quarter-circle around the puppy, then go back to the original point in front of him. Next, make a half-circle around him and back again, and finally, make a complete circle. Move clockwise first, and then counterclockwise.

Remember not to go too fast in this training. If your puppy starts to move or tries

Giving praise when the puppy masters "Stay."

"Stay" at a short distance.

to follow, you may be going too fast for him to understand, so back up to the point where he understands what you want him to do, and finish the session at that point. Let the puppy go and play or you can play with him, then come back and do another session.

Keep each training session short, proceeding one step at a time. Many small sessions are better than one long session. For a young dog to learn, *less* is definitely *more*.

Leading Exercises

Leading with Toys

> Enthusiastically call your puppy's name, adding a word like "Come," to get his attention. Holding a toy, walk forward, enticing him to come along with you. One choice is to use a ball or other toy attached to a string.

> As you keep walking, use the toy to attract your puppy to go with you and give him plenty of praise and treats. Start with just a few steps in the beginning, before releasing him and turning the session into play.

> After a play period, practice the same lead exercise as above, but this time use the toy to attract him to your opposite side.

Using a leading toy.

> Lay out a *Labyrinth* (p. 113) with poles, and walk through it with the dog at your side. For this exercise, besides a toy, it's helpful to have treats and a wand (see p. 95) with which you can guide the puppy along.

Leading on the Leash

When teaching your puppy to lead using a two-handed leash, it's best to work in the *Labyrinth* (p. 113). The predetermined boundaries create a visual orientation for you and the dog, making learning easier. Many dog-lovers and TTEAM practitioners worldwide find this method highly successful.

I suggest that you not only attach the leash to a flat collar, but also snap the other end to a dog harness (see p. 94): this allows you to send the dog subtle signals that have a positive effect on his balance. When you use a traditional leash attached only to the dog's collar, he's able to pull hard enough to injure the fragile vertebrae of his neck and put damaging pressure on his back, hips, and knees. Every time you allow your dog to pull, you are reinforcing the habit.

With the two-handed lead, you are both improving your own coordination and giving your dog a clear message. When leading your dog, hold the leashes loosely between thumb and forefinger. Hold your hands parallel with the thumbs up at a height that is comfortable for you. This enables you to give small, subtle and effective signals.

Indicate signals to stop, turn, and go by giving gentle, short pulses—alternately holding back and releasing. Make the signals clear and distinct. Stiff hands and arms lead a dog to pull, because he will react to strong pressure on the leash with counterpressure.

Leading with the Balance Leash

The concept behind the *Balance Leash* is to teach a puppy how to walk on a leash beside his owner, quietly and without pulling. The method places the center of

Putting on a dog harness, step-by-step.

gravity over the puppy's four legs, bringing a dog who has a tendency to pull back into balance.

Learning to walk quietly on a balance leash without pulling can prevent potential injury to the neck, back, hips, and knees of your puppy. Walking in balance without pulling is particularly important for dogs who tend toward hip dysplasia, or knee or neck weaknesses.

For the *Balance Leash*, the Tellington Method uses a "step-in" dog harness and a double-ended leash with snaps on both ends.

Here, the leash is fastened to the collar and dog harness.

> You'll need a "step-in" harness with a strap across the spine that has two rings for snapping on the leash. There is also a ring behind each shoulder and a loop or ring on the chest strap (see p. 94).

> You'll also use a 6-foot-long leash with small snaps on both ends (see p. 94).

How-To

Place your dog on your left and fasten the leash as follows:

> Guide one end of the leash from right to left, down through the chest ring or chest loop on the harness and fasten the leash snap onto the ring on the left shoulder strap.

> Take the other end of the leash and fasten the snap to the rings on top of the puppy's back.

> To maintain your puppy's attention and to correct his balance, guide him by lightly holding the leash in each hand.

> To slow or stop the puppy, give several gentle pulse-type signals alternating between one leash end and the other—i.e. the leash end attached to the chest and the one fastened to the of top of the dog harness. Be aware that your dog will stop in balance when you *release* rather than when you are tightening the leash. A common error is holding the leash pulled

The Balance Leash attached to a dog harness.

The Balance Leash with the Collar

If you are leading your puppy using a flat collar without a harness, fasten the leash in a way that prevents pulling.

> Stand on the right side of your dog; attach one end of the leash to the collar. Your left hand holds the leash away from the dog's neck.

Leading through the Labyrinth (p. 113).

tight even when the dog is standing still. Once the puppy has stopped, make sure that you have noticeable slack in the leash, and that you are in what we call the "neutral position."

When you are leading the dog and not signaling, the leash remains in neutral position with some slack at both contact points. A signal is initiated with a light contact followed by an immediate release on the leash to alert your dog. Now that he is alert, you can indicate what you want him to do, either verbally or with a movement of the leash.

> With your right hand, take up the other end of the leash and pull it behind the puppy's left elbow, bring it forward between his front legs and then take it up to the right side of the neck. Pull the leash upward to make sure that it is resting comfortably against the chest. If the puppy pulls, use the two-handed technique described on p. 106. If he walks along quietly beside you, hold the leash in your left hand only.

> To protect your puppy's fur and skin, use a soft leash with no rough edges.

Should your dog have a tendency to pull backward, I recommend using a dog harness with the balance leash (see p. 94).

Leading with the Halti Head Collar (or Snoot Loop)

In most cases, training conducted in the Playground for Higher Learning (p. 113) with the dog harness and *Balance Leash* will teach your puppy the necessary self-control to become a reliable and self-confident companion for you and your family. However, the Halti head collar is helpful if you have acquired a big, strong, difficult young dog who has not received basic training, reacts to other dogs with anxiety-provoked aggression, barks uncontrollably, or is hyperactive. When introduced with respect and care, the Halti can even change aggressive behavior.

I recommend the Halti head collar, or for dogs with short or broad muzzles, the Snoot Loop. You can also find many other brands and styles of canine halters on the market (see p. 94).

Generally, dogs who are in training with a Halti bring concentration and focus to their learning process. It's important that you introduce the Halti with the same care and respect that you use when initiating any training aid. Be sensitive and gentle and show your dog what you

Leading with a Halti: the leash is held with both hands in the neutral position.

expect from him. If possible, ask a two-legged partner to help you try out a few "dry run" exercises on yourself. This will give you a real sense of what the Halti feels like to your puppy. Take turns with your partner in wearing the Halti on your hands and leading each other through the *Labyrinth* (p. 113) or over obstacles. Give each other feedback. Discover what a gentle signal actually feels like. Keeping a clear sense of this feeling in mind will help you provide subtle signaling when you are leading your dog. Once you become sensitive in leading your human partner, you're ready to start training your dog.

I believe that just like TTouch, training with a Halti in the Playground for Higher Learning can release negative patterns, experiences, and traumas stored in the cells of the body—imprints of fear, pain, insecurity, nervousness, and hyperactivity. The latest research in cellular biology has shown that emotions—both negative and positive—are stored in the biochemistry of the body's cells.

Getting used to the Halti: At first, an elastic band is placed around the muzzle. Wearing the head collar is rewarded with a treat.

How-To

It's important to prepare a young dog for the Halti by accustoming him to it in stages. At first, wearing a strap around his nose will seem strange to him. The following steps are a helpful way to familiarize the puppy with his new canine halter.

> First, I put a simple elastic band around the dog's muzzle, to familiarize him with the feeling of something being there. I use the *Mouth TTouch* (p. 41) to promote his cooperation and to help him have a positive emotional response.

> When the dog has learned to accept the band around his muzzle, he's ready for the Halti. Make sure it's a comfortable fit. The nose strap should not be able to slide over the nose or the eyes. When the Halti or any other head collar is adjusted comfortably, you should be able to slide a finger under both sides of the jowl straps.

> The puppy should wear the Halti a few times every day without a leash and without being led. Once the puppy has accepted it, begin the lead training.

> Attach the leash to the harness and the Halti and lead the dog using both your hands (see p. 106). Hold the leash end that is fastened to the Halti loosely.

> Your puppy experiences your control mainly through the harness. The Halti is used to give him direction signals. If your dog behaves aggressively toward people or other dogs, you can calm him down by using the Halti to turn his head away.
> Lead the puppy through the *Labyrinth* and over obstacles (see p. 113).

Leading in the Labyrinth

Training in the *Labyrinth* (p. 113) is helpful in order to teach your puppy basic obedience. The boundary poles outlining the *Labyrinth* pathways help the puppy to concentrate and be goal-oriented.

The first time you lead the puppy in the *Labyrinth*, just take him through at his normal walking tempo. Then add the exercises for "Sit," and "Stay."

Take the puppy through the *Labyrinth* in both directions and lead him from both sides. To maintain the puppy's attention and interest, keep the periods of exercise short and have him work with other obstacles between sessions. Use the *Labyrinth* for "Sit," "Stay," and "Come," exercises: ask the puppy to "Sit," and "Stay," at one end of a *Labyrinth* pathway, and move a few steps away to the other end. Then call your dog to you.

It's beneficial to go through the *Labyrinth* with another friendly dog. Take the dogs in opposite directions as well as

Group training in the Labyrinth (p. 113) strengthens socialization.

toward each other. This exercise is very useful if your puppy is either timid or aggressive around other dogs. If you're working in the *Labyrinth* with another dog, watch the communication between the dogs to make sure that they are not stressed by working too close together. If you see that the work space is too small, create barriers to set the dogs apart, or make your *Labyrinth* wider.

Journey of the Homing Pigeon: A Leading Exercise Using Two People

This leading exercise with a person walking on either side of the dog is meant for dogs aged one year or older. In the Tellington Method we named this exercise *Journey of the Homing Pigeon* because the two people reminded me of outstretched wings. *Journey of the Homing Pigeon* has a focusing and calming effect on your dog because the two people create a sense of protection and safety. This exercise uses two leashes and there are many ways to make use of them depending on the size and age of your dog.

Because the neck muscles of a young dog are not yet fully developed, I suggest you use a dog harness for this leading exercise. The photo below illustrates how the leashes are fastened to the harness.

The two-person leading exercise is called Journey of the Homing Pigeon.

Here, the leashes are held taut in order for you to see the harness fastenings.

Each leash is run across the dog's chest and then snapped onto the ring on the opposite side. The leash on the right side is also attached to the ring on the top of the harness, so that the dog can receive gentle signals telling him to stop, turn, or slow down.

The exercises for the basic commands of "Sit," and "Down," can be taught in the Labyrinth (p. 113) using the wand.

Leading with the Wand

The wand (see p. 95) is used in the *Labyrinth* (p. 113) to playfully encourage the dog; by following it, he learns to walk on the leash. Hold the wand in front of the dog, using it to guide the way forward. You can also use the wand in the Playground for Higher Learning when working with obstacles (see p. 113). With some dogs, stroking the back and legs with the wand helps to heighten body awareness, but this doesn't always work, because some dogs just want to play with the wand.

If you have gone to an animal shelter to pick out a dog and find you like one who is afraid of contact, you can try touching him with the wand as a first encounter. However, if the dog has been abused, the wand might frighten him, in which case you should, of course, not use it.

> **>LINDA'S TIP**
>
> *The wand I use for training is white, stiff, and about 3 feet long. However, you can also use a rod with a little piece of cloth attached to one end.*

The Playground for Higher Learning

The Playground for Higher Learning is a great educational aid for your puppy. The course obstacles—such as the *Labyrinth* (see below) and the *Board* (p. 114)—are not overly demanding for your puppy, making the various exercises easy to master. Learning through working with a variety of obstacles teaches the young dog cooperation, concentration, and obedience, besides being fun and a change of pace for both you and your puppy.

> You'll discover that it's easier for both dogs and humans to concentrate on a task when they are presented with clear visual parameters.

> Remember to teach the exercises slowly, and keep the learning sessions short.

> As well as mastering the obstacles, the Playground for Higher Learning offers many opportunities to practice basic exercises like leading, "Sit," "Down," and "Stay."

> Use the pauses between sessions to TTouch your dog with the *Lying Leopard* (p. 28). TTouch promotes a puppy's learning ability and is also a good way to complete a lesson.

In the Playground for Higher Learning, puppies who are meant to become future show, work, sports, service, or rescue dogs receive valuable basic training that will prove useful for these later roles. Aside from being constructive, the training in the Playground for Higher Learning is a great deal of fun, especially when you train with other human-dog teams.

All the equipment for Playground for Higher Learning is easy to find as well as inexpensive. It can be used not only when your puppy is young, but also as he grows older, to keep him healthy and fit.

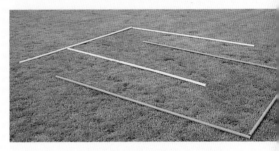

The paths of the Labyrinth measure about 3 feet across. This distance should be wider for larger dogs.

Labyrinth

Training in the *Labyrinth* offers the best means for your puppy to learn concentration and focus because it is so multifaceted. In the *Labyrinth*, you can teach your puppy all the basic requests he will need to understand, such as "Sit," "Down," "Stay," and how to lead.

To construct the *Labyrinth*, you need six plastic poles of about 1 to 3 inches in

TTouch practitioner Katja Krau (left) and Matthias Huber (second from the right) working in one of their puppy classes.

diameter and 4 yards in length. To transport and store the poles easily, you can divide them into 1-yard sections. Lengths of light plastic PVC pipe connected with fittings or connectors have proven to work well. You can also use these poles to create the pattern for the *Star* exercise (p. 118) or other ground exercises. Four extra poles can also be laid out to serve as an "entrance" and "exit," making it easier for your puppy to move into and out of the *Labyrinth*.

The Labyrinth at a Glance

> Promotes concentration

> Links and stimulates both hemispheres of the brain

> Presents boundaries for exercise pathways

> Works as a training space to teach leading from both sides

> Increases the flexibility of both sides of the body

> Acts as a training space for basic commands and obedience

> Can be easily constructed or removed in any location

Board

The *Board* exercise is a good way to improve your dog's concentration and balance. You begin by placing a wooden board on the ground. The standard *Board* should be about 10 inches wide, 10 feet long, and an inch thick. If your puppy is a small breed, use a smaller board. If the board is slippery, make it slide-proof by placing "cross-strips" every 10 inches. You can also cover it with a piece of carpet, which would allow the *Board* to also serve as a *Teeter-Totter* (p. 115).

Take a number of treats and lay them out on the *Board*, one every 4 inches. With the help of a wand, guide your puppy onto the *Board*. If he reacts nervously, take him across the *Board* sideways at first, and

Treats motivate and reward this young boxer.

The Board promotes balance and concentration.

then continue by walking him along the length in curving lines that cross at intervals rather than straight down it.

If your puppy is uncooperative or extremely anxious and refuses to step onto the *Board*, you can accustom him to it by placing two narrower boards in a "V" formation, gradually moving them together in the course of the training. In this way, an insecure dog can be slowly introduced to this exercise.

The next step for an "uncomplicated" puppy is to walk along a board that is slightly elevated above the ground. These

The Board at a Glance

> Promotes physical and emotional balance

> Promotes concentration

> Prepares for crossing bridges

> Can be converted to serve as a *Teeter-Totter* obstacle (see below)

> Serves as a preparation for agility, rescue, or service dog training

simple tasks promote self-confidence and awareness in your puppy.

Teeter-Totter (See-Saw)

If you add a fulcrum under the middle of the *Board*, it can double as a *Teeter-Totter*. For a start, I recommend that you make the *Teeter-Totter* no higher than 3 inches at its mid point. To make sure the *Teeter-Totter* is steady and safe, test it with your foot. Your puppy could become frightened if it suddenly tipped over. After your dog

Group training the Board exercise.

has gained experience and enjoys this exercise, you can make the *Teeter-Totter* higher.

Slalom

You may be familiar with the Slalom as an exercise used in agility training. It is great fun for both dogs and humans. At first, practice the Slalom with a leash and at a slow speed. Once the puppy has understood what you want him to do, you can speed up and finally even discard the leash.

You'll need five or six cones, poles, or other appropriate objects set up in a straight line. At first, the distance between each cone should be at least one-and-a-half times as long as your dog's body. With the help of a wand and a two-person lead, you can show your puppy where he is supposed to go. For this exercise, it's a good idea to train with other dogs—it's a lot more fun and the dogs learn from each other.

Two-person leading is a training technique for working with the Slalom.

Two kinds of slalom courses.

The Slalom at a Glance

> Increases focus and flexibility
> Prepares for agility training
> Can be practiced slow or fast
> Dog's love this exercise, once they understand it

Poles and Ladder

Poles

Use light plastic poles such as you use for the *Labyrinth* (p. 113), which you can raise with various supports to make a series of low "jumps," if you wish. (You can also use these to construct the *Star* on

p. 118.) You'll need two to six poles of about 6 feet in length. Don't place them too high—you want them low enough to encourage your puppy to jump.

The distance between the *Poles* is determined by the size and speed of your dog. Distance can vary between half your dog's body length and 3 feet.

To start with, lay the *Poles* flat on the ground. Walk over the *Poles* together with your dog so that he understands what you want him to do. You can use the wand and treats to entice and reward the puppy.

After a few times going over the *Poles* with your puppy, move so that you are on the outside of the obstacle but still next to your dog and accompanying him while he practices the exercise. It's helpful to perform this exercise with other dogs in order to socialize your puppy.

Ladder

For some dogs, the *Ladder* exercise can be

Wearing a T-Shirt (p. 88) gives a feeling of security to this young German shepherd.

a challenge at first. Each exercise influences a dog in a way that cannot be predicted.

To make a *Ladder* obstacle, lay a simple wooden or aluminum ladder on the ground. In mastering the *Ladder*, your dog learns to pay precise attention to the

Poles with cones.

The Ladder obstacle.

spaces between the rungs and to match his steps accordingly. If your puppy refuses to step between the rungs, lead him through in a serpentine pattern or get him to follow behind another dog. If your dog keeps jumping across the *Ladder*, awaken his interest in doing the exercise by putting treats in the spaces between each of the rungs.

If you see that your puppy is still a bit insecure about negotiating the Ladder, place it next to a wall or fence, thus creating a solid boundary on one side. The puppy will feel safer, and you will only need to control him from one side.

You can also lay out plain or multi-colored poles as a sort of "entranceway" in front of the Ladder. Lay them out in the shape of a "V" to show the dog the way to the start of the exercise.

If the puppy leaves the ladder in the middle of the exercise, lead him quietly back to it and guide him along again in a

"Very well done!"

The wand entices the young terrier.

serpentine pattern. Put treats in the spaces between the rungs.

Make sure that you advance the exercise slowly, step-by-step. Keep in mind that this is not only a workout, but a time for fun for you and your dog. Give him plenty of praise with your voice and with TTouch. And of course, if your puppy is shy or nervous, it's always good to have lots of treats on hand.

Star

The *Star* is an interesting obstacle be-

Poles and Ladder at a Glance

> Promotes skill and awareness
> Controls gait and length of stride
> Enhances muscle tone
> Improves the gait of future show dogs

cause the dog has to simultaneously step forward and bend his body a bit. If the poles are slightly raised, it can improve a dog's mobility even more. For a puppy, however, it's better to lay the poles flat on the ground so that he doesn't stress his spinal column.

The *Star* is composed of five poles, each 6 feet long, and laid out in a fan with one end of each meeting at a center point. Use the same methods you used in the *Poles and Ladder* (p. 116) to lead your puppy through the *Star*.

Ground Surfaces

Training your dog to tread on different types of surfaces is a useful preparation for everyday living. When you're taking a walk, shopping, or visiting someone with your puppy, you're likely to encounter grates, manholes, plastic mats, carpeted floors, and smooth tiles, to name a few. If you prepare the puppy well for such common situations, he will not find them stressful. While this training is valuable for all dogs, enabling them to walk securely and without fear on any surface, it is particularly valuable for puppies with future careers as therapy and rescue dogs.

Employ as many different surfaces as you can—for instance, fine wire mesh (window screening would be good) stapled to a frame; door mats; hard plastic that doesn't splinter and can simulate

Training in the Star.

Negotiating various surfaces.

>TTOUCH TIP

Paw TTouch, p. 46
Python TTouch, p. 34

Working with tires and hoops.

smooth tiles or icy surfaces; water puddles; plastic sheeting, and so on.

If you notice that your puppy is fearful or nervous, prepare him with the *Paw TTouch* (p. 46) or the *Python TTouch* (p. 34). When a dog is frightened his muscles tense, restricting circulation in his legs all the way down to his paws. As a result, the puppy's sense of his own legs and paws is dimmed. Use TTouches on the legs to restore feeling and circulation. In addition, put a *Body Wrap* (p. 87) or *T-Shirt* (p. 88) on him to help him feel more secure.

Hoops and Tires

One way to create circular obstacles is to use three to six plastic hula hoops that you can buy in a toy store. How you arrange the hoops on the ground can vary: you can lay them out in a row, place them around in a circle, or put them one on top of the other like pick-up-sticks, so that the puppy must try to find his way through them. You can also stand them up on their sides for a different look.

Tires are more difficult for the puppy to master. You'll need a few discarded auto, motorcycle, or bicycle tires, which you lay out in a row. To start with, put treats into the empty center of the tire where the puppy can see them. This will motivate the puppy to first look into the tire center and eventually to step inside it.

Hoops and Tires at a Glance

> Stepping into hoops and tires promotes concentration and alertness

> They can be used in a variety of ways

Dog Dancing

If you're looking for fun for you and your puppy, try *Dog Dancing*. Dancing to music with a dog (some people call it "canine freestyle") has become really popular in the last few years. It's an amusing activity, and at the same time it boosts a puppy's intelligence, mobility, and cooperation. It's also a great way to train the puppy the basics, such as "Sit," "Stay," and "Come."

Dog Dancing can be practiced with dogs of all ages, in any venue regardless of the weather.

TTouch practitioner Karin Petra Freiling demonstrates five dance exercises that can be learned by everyone. They are playful and easy for puppies to do. However, as you learn them keep in mind that jumping, and walking or standing on the hind legs can be harmful for young dogs who are still in their formative growth phase, and we do not recommend such exercise until your dog is older.

It's important that a puppy feels motivated to begin the *Dog Dancing* exercises. Use his favorite treats and toys and let him know in a warm and friendly voice what you want from him. These are exercises that can definitely be a joy for all involved. However, though you may be having a great time, limit the session to a few minutes and make sure to end it on a good note.

Reminder: TTouch is very good as a warm-up and relaxant (see pp. 24–46).

Offering the Paw

Offering the Paw is a lovely exercise which you can use as a prelude to *Dog Dancing*. The puppy learns to raise one of his paws and lay it in your hand. *Offering the Paw* is natural behavior for puppies: they use it when begging for food from an older animal.

How-To

Kneel down beside your dog and hold a treat in your closed hand. The puppy should be allowed to sniff but not eat it.

With two, training your puppy is double the fun.

Timmy offers his paw.

He'll try to somehow get at this tasty delight. Mostly, he'll sit down, especially if he already knows the voice cue of his name and "Sit." When "sitting" doesn't give him the goodie he is longing for, he'll probably revert to his instinctive way of begging for food and raise his paw. As soon as he does, you must be instantly alert and say, "Good paw," or "Give me five," or "Helloooo," or whatever voice cue you want to consistently use in the future.

At the same time, gently put your hand under his paw without holding it, and with your other hand, give him the treat he has earned. Some puppies put their paw right onto the hand in which you are holding the treat, in which case you can give the treat and the voice signal at the same time. Hold the paw gently in your free hand, but only after the puppy has raised it.

Paw TTouches (p. 46) are a helpful preparation for this exercise.

If the training works with one paw, it's nice to do the same with the other one, using a different voice signal this time, like, "Give me ten."

If the puppy masters this skill, you can play other games later, like *Stepping*. For this, the human and the dog stand opposite each other and the dog uses his paw to tap the foot of the person. Or you can have your puppy wave, a delightful ending to a successful dance session or a friendly goodbye to visitors.

The Circle

In the *Circle*, the puppy runs once around the human. This is one of the easiest dance exercises. With the help of a reward treat, entice your dog to circle around your legs so that he does so one or more times.

How-To

As the puppy sits in front of you, hold a treat in your right hand at his nose level. Moving your hand to the right, entice him to come around to your right side.

When he has made a quarter of a circle around you, reward him with a treat. On your next attempt, reward him after he has gone a bit further, and so on until he has completed a circle. When he's reached a point behind your back, it's easier to switch the treat to your left hand. It's important to go slowly, step-by-small-step.

Consistently give him the same voice signals, for example, "Circle, please."

Forming a clear mental picture of each step in the exercise is very helpful. Our experience has shown that dogs apparently perceive our mental images. Imagine each small step the puppy is to perform, and only after he has progressed through them, picture him mastering the full circle.

Practice the *Circle* in both directions in order to address both sides of the puppy's body equally. Think of a different voice signal for the changed direction, for instance, "Round, please."

Later, the dog will be able to circle not only you, but also (for example) a tree, an umbrella, or another dog. This exercise can actually be useful—if the dog has wrapped his leash around an object like a lamppost, you can easily disentangle him by asking him to "Circle."

The Figure Eight

In this exercise, which is an expansion of the *Circle*, the dog walks a figure eight around your legs. The puppy moves through your spread legs from the back to the front, proceeds around the outside of one leg, then back through your legs again, and finally once more around the outside of your other leg.

Timmy receives a treat at different points while learning the Circle exercise.

Timmy is led once around the right leg.

At the end of the Figure Eight, Timmy has come around the left leg.

How-To

Again, offering treats is a key to learning the exercise. Holding a treat in your right hand, lure the puppy to come through your outspread legs from the back to the front. Then, still using the treat as a lure, bring him around your right leg. Here he receives the treat he has earned. Now, with a treat in your left hand, move it between your legs to attract the puppy to the front again and then around your left leg. From here, your right hand takes over again as treat benefactor. It's a good idea to have treats at the ready in each hand.

It's helpful to try a "dry run" without your dog first. When the exercise is clear to you in both theory and practice, you'll be ready to work on it with your puppy.

The voice cue here could be, for example, "Slaaaaa ......Looooom, please," "Sla," for the movement around the first leg, and "Lom," for the second.

The Spin

The *Spin* is a dog pirouette in which the puppy turns on his own axis once or several times, beside, behind, or in front of you.

How-To

The photo series illustrates how to use treats to motivate the dog to perform the *Spin*. It's important to hold the treat by the puppy's nose as he's standing. Some dogs immediately lie down if the treat is held too low; others sit when it's held to far over the back. Test this to discover the ideal height for your dog.

Next, slowly bring the treat to a position at the root of the puppy's tail. If he follows the movement, give him his treat as he is turning his head. The next goodie comes to him when he follows the treat to a position at the middle of his spine, then once more when the treat is at the root of the tail again, and so forth.

Gradually reduce the number of treats used. Introduce voice cues from the outset—for instance, "Spiiiin, please." Once he gets the exercise in one direction down pat, go in the other direction. Change the voice cue for this direction to something like, "Oooother way, please."

Rollover

From the "Down" position, you can show your puppy that you want him to turn over on his back and then rollover from there until he's back in the "Down" position. Rolling is part of a dog's instinctive behavior. Perhaps you've observed it in action when your little rascal rolls around on his back while playing with a toy.

How-To

Begin with the puppy lying down on his stomach. Saying "Rollover, please," and using a treat, entice him to turn his head to the side and back toward his shoulder, and then give him his first treat. In the

Gordon follows the treat curiously. He's rewarded, first after half a Spin, and then after a full one.

The puppy turns his head and Karin immediately rewards him. Imke does the Raccoon TTouch (p. 30): now we're halfway there. The Rollover is a success—time to party!

next step, lead him a little bit further in the direction of his spine. Now the dog will have rolled onto his side, and you can feed him the second treat.

Follow this by holding a treat up over the dog's nose and moving it so that he'll roll over onto his back. Then give him the next reward from the side, so that he rolls back into the "Down" position. Success! Now is the time to play and make a huge fuss over your puppy so he'll enjoy doing the exercise again.

Train the puppy to do the entire exercise in the other direction as well, using a different cue, such as, "Roll next, please."

Tips for Dog Dancing Training

> Direction: To begin with, train your puppy in these exercises in one direction only, so as not to confuse him. Once he really knows the movements in one direction, you can change over and teach him the other.
> It's a good idea to divide complex exercises into small steps, giving puppies a chance to proceed at their own personal pace. Every learning success, no matter how small, should be acknowledged and celebrated. If there's a problem with moving on to a new step, just return to the easier ones that the puppy has already learned and finish the lesson with a big reward of praise and treats. This en-

courages your young friend to return to the next training session with renewed enthusiasm.

> Practice sessions should not last long, but rather should occur a number of times a day.

> Of course, all these exercises can also be practiced very well using Clicker Training. You'd be well advised to attend a Clicker Training course to make sure that you are not teaching your dog confusing signals (see p. 131).

> To optimize your dog's concentration and learning capacity, take him through some ground exercises in the *Labyrinth* (p. 113) before attempting the *Dog Dancing* exercises.

> Should the dog seem overactive and unfocused, *Noah's March* (p. 37), connected *Lying Leopard TTouches* (p. 28) over the whole body, the *Body Wrap* (p. 87), and *Ear TTouches* (p. 42) are calming and helpful.

Appendix

Acknowledgments

Dedication

To my brilliant sister, Robyn Hood,
who has been so instrumental
in spreading TTouch around the world,
and
to my husband, Roland Kleger,
in gratitude for his love, his support and
his talent at knowing just the right word when I am stuck.

Many people contributed to the making of this book. It would not have taken form without the dedication, expertise, and writing skill of my co-author, Gudrun Braun. Thank you, Gudrun, in the name of all the puppies and their people who I know will benefit from integrating TTouch into their lives. I'm so grateful for the delightful photos by Gabriele Metz, and also for her extensive contacts in the dog world. She put out the call to puppy owners who traveled from many parts of Germany with their families and friends to spend the day with us at the photo shoot. And thanks to her partner, Marc Heppner, for his part in the shoot and for bringing the sun after two weeks of steady rain.

I feel so blessed that Sybil Taylor, my co-author on three previous books, agreed to translate this puppy book from the original German. She brings charm and a lovely tone to every book she touches.

My deep appreciation goes to Kirsten Henry for the hours we spent together checking all the details and for her dedication to perfect translations from English for the German edition of this book.

Many thanks go to the following TTouch practitioners for their valuable contributions: Australian TTouch Practitioner and dog trainer, Andy Robertson, for such a caring and successful method of teaching the art of good canine citizenship—"Sit, Come, Stay"; Karin Freiling, for her suggestions and patient review of the text, and the Dog Dancing exercises and photographs; Austrian TTouch Practitioner and veterinarian, Dr. Martina Simmerer, for her guidance on nutrition for your puppies; British Dog Behaviorist and TTouch Practitioner, Sarah Marsh, for her advice and expertise on the importance of introducing and supervising puppies in play groups.

My special thanks go to Caroline Robbins and Martha Cook of Trafalgar Square Books for their support and promotion of TTEAM and TTouch over so many years.

Sarah Marsh with Doodle. Kirsten Henry and Jessie.

We had the use of two excellent venues. My thanks to TTouch Practitioners Katja Kruaß and Matthias Huber for their assistance in organizing the photo shoot for part of this book. They did an excellent job of gathering clients from their GREH dog school for the filming at their beautifully equipped Berlin facility.

This work would never have spread around the world as it has without the support, advice, and skill of my sister, Robyn Hood. I am deeply appreciative to her and to our other TTouch instructors, Edie Jane Eaton, Debby Potts, Kathy Cascade, Sarah Fisher, and Bibi Degn for their dedication to teaching this work. I want to acknowledge and thank our international organizers: Bibi Degn in Germany, Sarah Fisher in the UK, Martin Lasser in Austria, Teresa Cottarelli and Doris Süess in Switzerland, and Eugenie Chopin in South Africa.

I want to thank also our talented, marvelous group of certified TTEAM and TTouch teachers in 26 countries who give workshops and do individual work with many species of companion animals. They're "Changing the World, One TTouch at a Time." You can check out our website at www.ttouch.com to find a TTouch teacher in your area.

These acknowledgements would not be complete without honoring all the puppies who have brought so much joy to my life, and to those who enrich the lives of each one of you.

Robyn Hood and Roy.

My heartfelt thanks go to all the people who have embraced the philosophy of TTouch and to you, dear Reader. May this book bring you new appreciation of your animals as well as a deeper understanding of our human species, and gift you with a means of finding special ways of guiding your puppy to be all she, or he, can be.

Linda Tellington Jones

Further Reading

Books
by Linda Tellington-Jones *

1992: *The Tellington TTouch: A Revolutionary Natural Method to Train and Care for Your Favorite Animal* by Linda Tellington-Jones with Sybil Taylor. Viking Penguin Group

1995: *Getting In TTouch: Understand and Influence Your Horse's Personality* by Linda Tellington-Jones with Sybil Taylor. Trafalgar Square Books

1997: *Let's Ride! With Linda Tellington-Jones: Fun and TTeamwork with your Horse or Pony* by Linda Tellington-Jones and Andrea Pabel. Trafalgar Square Books (First published as *Die Linda Tellington-Jones Reit Schule*. Kosmos)

1999: *Improve Your Horse's Well-Being* by Linda Tellington-Jones. Trafalgar Square Books

2001: *Getting In TTouch with Your Dog: How to Influence Behavior, Health and Performance* by Linda Tellington-Jones. Trafalgar Square Books (First published in German in as *Tellington-Training fur Hunde*. Kosmos)

2003: *Getting In TTouch with Your Cat: A New and Gentle Way to Harmony, Behavior and Well-Being* by Linda Tellington-Jones. Trafalgar Square Books (First published in German as *TTouch fur Katzen*. Kosmos)

2003: *TTouch for You! Gesundheit und Wohlgefuehl mit dem Tellington TTouch* by Linda Tellington-Jones and Sybil Taylor (Currently available only in German. Kosmos)

2006: *The Ultimate Horse Behavior and Training Book: Enlightened and Revolutionary Solutions for the 21st Century* by Linda Tellington-Jones with Bobbie Lieberman. Trafalgar Square Books

*Several of these books are published in other languages: Czechoslovakian, Danish, Flemish, French, German, Italian, Japanese, Norwegian, Russian, Spanish, and Swedish

Videos**

Unleash Your Dogs Potential by Linda Tellington-Jones. Trafalgar Square Books. DVD

**For an additional list of 12 videos go to www.ttouch.com

Additional Recommended Reading

After You Get Your Puppy by Dr. Ian Dunbar. James & Kenneth Publishers

Dr Dunbar's Good Little Dog Book by Dr. Ian Dunbar. James & Kenneth Publishers

Getting Started: Clicker Training for Dogs by Karen Pryor. Sunshine Books

On Talking Terms with Dogs: Calming Signals by Turid Rugaas. Dogwise Publishing

Useful Addresses

USA
Tellington TTouch Training
Linda Tellington-Jones
P.O. Box 3793, Santa Fe, NM 87501
Phone: 800 854 8326
E-mail: info@tellingtontraining.com
www.ttouch.com

CANADA
Robyn Hood
3435 Rochdell Road
Vernon, British Columbia V1B 3E8
Phone: 250 545 2336
E-mail: ttouch@shaw.ca
www.tteam-ttouch.ca

UNITED KINGDOM
Sarah Fisher
Tilley Farm, Timsbury Rd.,
Farmborough, nr Bath
Somerset BA2 0AB
Phone: 44 1761 471182
Fax: 44 1761 479082
E-mail: sarahfisher@tteam.co.uk
www.ttouchteam.co.uk

SOUTH AFRICA
Eugenie Chopin
P.O Box 729
Strathaven 2031
Phone: 27 11 884 3156
Fax: 27 11 783 1515
E-mail: info@ttouchsa.co.za
www.ttouchsa.co.za

AUSTRALIA
Andy Robertson
28 Calderwood Rd
Gaiston NSW 02159
Phone: 61 2 9653 3507
Fax: 61 2 9653 3507
E-mail: ttouch@cia.com.au

GERMANY
Bibi Degn
Hassel 4
D-57589 Pracht
Phone: 49 2682 8886
Fax: 49 2682 6683
E-mail: info@tteam.de
www.tteam.de

AUSTRIA
Martin Lasser
Spitalgasse 7
A – 2540 Bad Voeslau
Phone: 43 664 125 0252
E-mail: tteam.office@aon.at
www.tteam.at

SWITZERLAND
Kirsten Bollinger
Via Suot Chesas 3
CH- 7512 Champfer
Phone: 41 81 834 4178
E-mail: gilde@tteam.ch
www.tteam.ch

ITALY
E-mail: info@tteam.it
www.tteam.it

NETHERLANDS
E-mail: marjolein@ttouch.nl
www.gsd.nl

Index

Page numbers in *italics* indicate photographs or illustrations.